C000201649

2018 SQA Past Papers with Answers

Higher
GERMAN

FREE
audio files to accompany this title can
be accessed at
**www.hoddereducation.co.uk/
sqaaudiofiles**
You will find the files listed by
language and level.

2016, 2017 & 2018 Exams

Hodder Gibson Study Skills Advice – Higher German   – page 3
Hodder Gibson Study Skills Advice – General   – page 7
2016 EXAM   – page 9
2017 EXAM   – page 35
2018 EXAM   – page 63
ANSWERS   – page 89

HODDER
GIBSON
AN HACHETTE UK COMPANY

This book contains the official 2016, 2017 and 2018 Exams for Higher German, with associated SQA-approved answers modified from the official marking instructions that accompany the paper.

In addition the book contains skills advice. This advice has been specially commissioned by Hodder Gibson, and has been written by experienced senior teachers and examiners in line with the new Higher syllabus and assessment outlines. This is not SQA material but has been devised to provide further guidance for Higher examinations.

Every effort has been made to trace the copyright holders and to obtain their permission for the use of copyright material. Hodder Gibson will be happy to receive information allowing us to rectify any error or omission in future editions.

Hachette UK's policy is to use papers that are natural, renewable and recyclable products and made from wood grown in sustainable forests. The logging and manufacturing processes are expected to conform to the environmental regulations of the country of origin.

Orders: please contact Bookpoint Ltd, 130 Park Drive, Milton Park, Abingdon, Oxon OX14 4SE. Telephone: (44) 01235 827827. Fax: (44) 01235 400454. Lines are open 9.00–5.00, Monday to Saturday, with a 24-hour message answering service. Visit our website at www.hoddereducation.co.uk. Hodder Gibson can also be contacted directly at hoddergibson@hodder.co.uk

This collection first published in 2018 by
Hodder Gibson, an imprint of Hodder Education,
An Hachette UK Company
211 St Vincent Street
Glasgow G2 5QY

Typeset by Aptara, Inc.

Printed in the UK

A catalogue record for this title is available from the British Library

ISBN: 978-1-5104-5666-2

2 1

2019 2018

MIX
Paper from
responsible sources
FSC
www.fsc.org   FSC™ C104740

Introduction

Higher German

Well done for choosing to add Higher German to your now-growing list of qualifications! As you know, German is the most spoken language in Europe and is rising in importance around the world, especially for business, tourism, science and research. Whatever plans you have for the future, rest assured that knowledge of German will increase your options.

What can Higher German do for you?

The Higher German course has been developed to follow on from the National 5 qualification in order to prepare you for an ever-competitive global job market.

The aim of this course is to develop your linguistic skills and cultural awareness through understanding (reading and listening) and using (talking and writing) detailed and complex language through the following contexts:

- **society** (family and friends, lifestyle, media, global languages, citizenship)
- **learning** (learning in context and education)
- **employability** (jobs, work and CVs)
- **culture** (planning a trip, other countries, celebrating a special event, German literature, German film and television)

What does the course assessment look like?

The exam at Higher German follows on naturally from National 5. The Higher exam allows you to demonstrate your ability to understand and use detailed and complex language in German.

There are many aspects of the Higher German exam that are similar to the National 5 exam.

In National 5, there were three reading texts of 200 words and at Higher there will be one text of 600 words, including a translation.

Just like at National 5, there will be a monologue and a dialogue in the listening.

The biggest difference between National 5 and Higher is in the writing elements. The level of predictability of the National 5 Writing is lower at Higher and you will have to respond to unseen topics. This means that you will need a good range of vocabulary and grammatical structures to tackle the assessment. Furthermore, the language is more complex and detailed throughout.

Reading/Directed Writing

This part of the exam will consist of two papers: Reading/Translation and Directed Writing. You will have 2 hours to complete all parts of both papers. These papers are worth 50 marks.

Listening

You will have 30 minutes to complete this paper. This paper is worth 20 marks

Talking

You will take part in a conversation of approximately 10 minutes with your teacher covering at least two contexts from the Higher Course. You will also be given marks for your ability to hold a natural conversation. This is worth 30 marks.

Assignment Writing

The Assignment (Writing) is part of the overall course assessment at Higher. It has a total mark allocation of 20 marks.

As part of the course work, you will produce a piece of discursive writing of about 200 to 250 words **independently** in German in class and over time.

Your teacher might provide you with a choice of writing stimuli in English which have been published by the SQA. However, your teacher might also give you writing stimuli that complement the course work or your teacher could ask you to come up with your own ideas for your assignment and support you to make the right choice.

Please note that in contrast to the Assignment Writing at National 5 you are expected to **write discursively and draw conclusions.**

What you have to do

The Reading and Translation

The reading section of this paper will have 30 marks – 20 marks for the text and 10 marks for the translation section.

You will read one German text of around 600 words and answer the questions which follow **in English**. The questions will test your ability to pick out complex and detailed information. There will be an **overall purpose question** and you will have to give reasons for your answer **with reference to the text**.

What is the "overall purpose"?

As you are a more advanced learner of German, you will be asked to read between the lines of the text that you have in front of you. Authors always have a message and all texts are produced for a reason and an audience, for example, to amuse, to persuade someone to vote, to raise concerns, to advertise, to give an opinion. Remember, at Higher you will need to refer to the text to justify your answer.

Within the Reading paper, you will be asked to translate a small section, which will be underlined, into English. This will assess your ability to look closely at the text and to produce a coherent translation in English.

You may use a dictionary in this section.

Directed Writing

The directed writing section of this paper worth 20 marks will give you two options to choose from. Please note that you only need to answer **ONE** of these questions. You will be given a scenario of a recent visit you have made to a German-speaking country with six bullet points. **It is important that you address every aspect of each bullet point.**

Remember that you are in control of the writing and can expand on each bullet point the way that you want to. Each bullet point is flexible so that you can demonstrate what you can do.

The text that you have to produce will be written mostly in the past tense and should be around 120–150 words.

You may use a dictionary in this section.

Listening

The listening section is worth 20 marks (20% of the overall mark).

There are two parts to this section. Firstly, you will hear a monologue (approximately 2 minutes) and then, a short dialogue (approximately 3 minutes) in German.

The monologue is worth 8 marks.

The dialogue is worth 12 marks and is thematically linked to the monologue.

Talking

The talking section features a conversation between you and your German teacher. Your German teacher will assess this section and will be able to help you prepare well in advance. It will be recorded for the SQA and marked by your teacher.

The conversation in German will be on topics from at least two Higher Course contexts:

- Society: friends, lifestyle choices, spare time
- Learning: school career, future plans, apprenticeship or university
- Employability: work experience, part-time job, working abroad
- Culture: a holiday abroad, a gap year, a favourite book or film

The conversation should last between 8 to 10 minutes. You may use some notes (not whole sentences or paragraphs).

The conversation is worth 30 marks and it is important to note that it should sound natural and spontaneous, rather than rehearsed.

Tips for success at Higher German

First and foremost, it is important that you don't panic! Keep calm and remember that you are demonstrating what you know to the examiner.

Remember to plan in advance – create a study timetable when you know when your exams are and plan your revision. An important point to remember is to learn vocabulary little and often. Make flash cards, or there are apps – such as Quizlet and Flashcards+ – for your smartphone, to help you!

Reading tips

Before you read the text:

- Read the introduction at the beginning of the text so you know what the text is about.
- Read the title if there is one – what do you know about the topic so far?
- Read the questions to help you anticipate what may come up in the text.
- Check to see if there is a glossary – no point looking up words that are given to you!

While reading the text:

- Quickly skim the text to get a feel for the structure.
- Focus – don't just stare at the words.
- Use your knowledge about language to work out the meanings of words by:
    - remembering some words have many meanings – does it fit in the context?
    - recognising if the word is a cognate or a near cognate (words that are similar in both German and English)
    - using the dictionary with care!

After you have read the text:

- Read the comprehension questions carefully.
- Underline the question word and circle the number of points to highlight what information and how many points the examiner is looking for.
- Make sure that you give as much detail as possible – again look at the number of marks. At Higher, the examiner is looking for detailed answers so check before and after your answer in the text to see if you have missed anything.
- Do not give alternatives – commit to your answer.
- Remember that the translation will **not** contain an answer to the comprehension questions – skim over it to save time.

When working on the translation section:

- Only attempt the translation after having read the text.
- Ensure that you accurately translate the words – watch out for separable verbs!
- Know what tense your verbs are in.
- Make sure you convey the meaning in good English.
- Do **NOT** miss out any words.

After you have answered the questions:

- Check your answers – read the question first and then your response – does it answer the question?
- Make sure that your answers in English make sense and your English is of a good standard.

Directed Writing tips

Before you sit your Directed Writing exam:

- Make sure you are familiar with the *Perfekt* and *Imperfekt* tenses.
- Practise writing different types of scenarios.
- Prepare a bank of phrases which you can use to impress the examiner.
- Read through the whole scenario carefully.
- Plan and structure your essay – leave enough time to check it.

During the Directed Writing exam:

- Write legibly so that the examiner can read what you've written.
- Set the scene – give an introduction of where you went and how you got there (even if it's not a bullet point!)
- Tick off the bullet points as you complete them.
- Ensure you convey the scenario accurately.
- Restrict your use of the dictionary to looking up keywords required to convey the message in the scenario and to check spelling and genders of what you have already written.

- Avoid translating from English to German – you will end up using English grammar.
- Remember you are encouraged to give any other details – so feel free to add any of those phrases you have prepared.
- Time yourself – try to restrict the time spent writing to 40 minutes.

After you have finished writing:

- Check you have covered all the bullet points (some bullet points have more than one part!).
- Go back through and check your grammar and spelling:
    - does your *Perfekt* construction have a subject, auxiliary verb and a past participle? e.g. *Ich habe gesehen, ich bin geflogen*
    - have you used the correct form *sein/haben* with your *Perfekt* construction?
    - check the genders of nouns
    - agreements – verbs and adjectives
    - cases – dative or accusative?
    - do all the nouns have capital letters?
- Check that your writing makes sense!

Listening tips

It is important that you regularly learn your vocabulary so that you are able to recognise words and phrases. Develop a system to help you do this: make flashcards, use vocabulary apps on your smartphone or online, use internet sites such as *YouTube* to listen to contemporary German, or even ask a family member to test you.

Before you sit your Listening exam:

- Revise vocabulary, especially verbs in different tense forms, quantifiers (*viel, wenig, die meisten*), numbers and dates. Read vocabulary out loud so that you can recognise how it sounds.
- Read the introduction and think about what you know about the topic.
- Remember to listen for cognates and near-cognates.
- Remember that practice makes perfect.
- Read the questions in English carefully – you are given time to study them before the text starts – underline question words and anticipate what type of answers you are listening for.
- Remember that the questions come in the same order as the text.

While you are sitting your Listening exam:

- You will hear both items (monologue and dialogue) twice so you don't need to get all the details on the first go.
- Make sure the examiner can see your final answer.
- If you don't understand a word, you need to use the context to help work it out or find a logical answer.
- Look at how many marks are allocated to the question – this will guide how much you need to write.
- Try to give as much detail as possible.

After your Listening exam:

- Look over your answers – make sure what you've written in English makes sense.
- Use a single line to strike through notes or draft answers.

Essay writing tips for the Assignment Writing

You will write a first draft that the teacher will provide general feedback on – which means the teacher cannot correct your errors. You should be able to improve the accuracy of your writing based on the teacher's feedback and a dictionary.

Before you sit your Writing exam:

- Read the stimulus carefully.
- Remember what you have learned on this topic in class.
- Remember discursive phrases and conclusions in German. **Learn them by heart if necessary.**
- Plan and structure your essay and leave enough time to check it.

During the writing (first and final draft):

- Write legibly so that the examiner can read what you've written.
- Write an introduction.
- Keep checking the stimulus to make sure you write to the topic.
- Use essay phrases and connectors to make your writing more interesting.
- Ensure you convey your ideas clearly and accurately.
- Restrict your use of the dictionary to looking up keywords and to checking spelling and genders of what you have already written.
- Avoid translating from English to German – you will end up using English grammar.

After you have finished writing:

- Check you have written to the topic.
- Go back through and check your grammar and spelling:
    - verb endings
    - check the genders of nouns
    - agreements – verbs and adjectives
    - cases – dative or accusative?
    - do all the nouns have capital letters?
- Check that your writing makes sense!

Good luck!

Remember that the rewards for passing Higher German are well worth it! Your pass will help you get the future you want for yourself. In the exam, be confident in your own ability. If you're not sure how to answer a question, trust your instincts and just give it a go anyway – keep calm and don't panic! GOOD LUCK!

Study Skills – what you need to know to pass exams!

General exam revision: 20 top tips

When preparing for exams, it is easy to feel unsure of where to start or how to revise. This guide to general exam revision provides a good starting place, and, as these are very general tips, they can be applied to all your exams.

1. Start revising in good time.

Don't leave revision until the last minute – this will make you panic and it will be difficult to learn. Make a revision timetable that counts down the weeks to go.

2. Work to a study plan.

Set up sessions of work spread through the weeks ahead. Make sure each session has a focus and a clear purpose. What will you study, when and why? Be realistic about what you can achieve in each session, and don't be afraid to adjust your plans as needed.

3. Make sure you know exactly when your exams are.

Get your exam dates from the SQA website and use the timetable builder tool to create your own exam schedule. You will also get a personalised timetable from your school, but this might not be until close to the exam period.

4. Make sure that you know the topics that make up each course.

Studying is easier if material is in manageable chunks – why not use the SQA topic headings or create your own from your class notes? Ask your teacher for help on this if you are not sure.

5. Break the chunks up into even smaller bits.

The small chunks should be easier to cope with. Remember that they fit together to make larger ideas. Even the process of chunking down will help!

6. Ask yourself these key questions for each course:

- Are all topics compulsory or are there choices?
- Which topics seem to come up time and time again?
- Which topics are your strongest and which are your weakest?

Use your answers to these questions to work out how much time you will need to spend revising each topic.

7. Make sure you know what to expect in the exam.

The subject-specific introduction to this book will help with this. Make sure you can answer these questions:

- How is the paper structured?
- How much time is there for each part of the exam?
- What types of question are involved? These will vary depending on the subject so read the subject-specific section carefully.

8. Past papers are a vital *revision tool!*

Use past papers to support your revision wherever possible. This book contains the answers and mark schemes too – refer to these carefully when checking your work. Using the mark scheme is useful; even if you don't manage to get all the marks available first time when you first practise, it helps you identify how to extend and develop your answers to get more marks next time – and of course, in the real exam.

9. Use study methods that work well for you.

People study and learn in different ways. Reading and looking at diagrams suits some students. Others prefer to listen and hear material – what about reading out loud or getting a friend or family member to do this for you? You could also record and play back material.

10. There are three tried and tested ways to make material stick in your long-term memory:

- Practising – e.g. rehearsal, repeating
- Organising – e.g. making drawings, lists, diagrams, tables, memory aids
- Elaborating – e.g. incorporating the material into a story or an imagined journey

11. Learn actively.

Most people prefer to learn actively – for example, making notes, highlighting, redrawing and redrafting, making up memory aids, or writing past paper answers. A good way to stay engaged and inspired is to mix and match these methods – find the combination that best suits you. This is likely to vary depending on the topic or subject.

12. Be an expert.

Be sure to have a few areas in which you feel you are an expert. This often works because at least some of them will come up, which can boost confidence.

13. Try some visual methods.

Use symbols, diagrams, charts, flashcards, post-it notes etc. Don't forget – the brain takes in chunked images more easily than loads of text.

14. Remember – practice makes perfect.

Work on difficult areas again and again. Look and read – then test yourself. You cannot do this too much.

15. Try past papers against the clock.

Practise writing answers in a set time. This is a good habit from the start but is especially important when you get closer to exam time.

16. Collaborate with friends.

Test each other and talk about the material – this can really help. Two brains are better than one! It is amazing how talking about a problem can help you solve it.

17. Know your weaknesses.

Ask your teacher for help to identify what you don't know. Try to do this as early as possible. If you are having trouble, it is probably with a difficult topic, so your teacher will already be aware of this – most students will find it tough.

18. Have your materials organised and ready.

Know what is needed for each exam:

- Do you need a calculator or a ruler?
- Should you have pencils as well as pens?
- Will you need water or paper tissues?

19. Make full use of school resources.

Find out what support is on offer:

- Are there study classes available?
- When is the library open?
- When is the best time to ask for extra help?
- Can you borrow textbooks, study guides, past papers, etc.?
- Is school open for Easter revision?

20. Keep fit and healthy!

Try to stick to a routine as much as possible, including with sleep. If you are tired, sluggish or dehydrated, it is difficult to see how concentration is even possible. Combine study with relaxation, drink plenty of water, eat sensibly, and get fresh air and exercise – all these things will help more than you could imagine. Good luck!

HIGHER

2016

National Qualifications 2016

X734/76/11

German Reading

WEDNESDAY, 1 JUNE
9:00 AM — 10:40 AM

Total marks — 30

Attempt ALL questions.

Write your answers clearly, in **English**, in the Reading Answer Booklet provided. In the answer booklet you must clearly identify the question number you are attempting.

You may use a German dictionary.

Use **blue** or **black** ink.

There is a separate question and answer booklet for Directed Writing. You must complete your answer for Directed Writing in the question and answer booklet for Directed Writing.

Before leaving the examination room you must give your Reading Answer Booklet and your Directed Writing question and answer booklet to the Invigilator; if you do not, you may lose all the marks for this paper.

Total marks — 30

Attempt ALL questions

Read the whole article carefully and then answer, in **English**, ALL the questions that follow.

While reading an online German magazine, you come across an article about how young people like to learn.

Die Freude am Lernen ist der Schlüssel zum Erfolg. Wenn das Lernen den Schulkindern Spaß macht, lernen sie schneller und besser.

Laut einer neuen Studie im Jugendmagazin „Zeit Leo" haben die meisten Schüler an deutschen Schulen nicht immer Spaß am Lernen. Während Schüler in der Grundschule
5 noch zu 53 Prozent der Meinung sind, dass das Lernen Spaß macht, sagen das nur sechs Prozent der 13-Jährigen.

Michael Felten, Lehrer am Schiller-Gymnasium in Düsseldorf, erklärt das Ergebnis der Studie: „Diese Lern-Unlust ist nichts Neues. Ich selbst habe im Laufe meiner langen Karriere viele Schüler gesehen, die in der Grundschule recht motiviert waren. Später
10 jedoch, in der Sekundarschule, waren genau dieselben Schüler demotiviert und haben sich nicht mehr im Unterricht bemüht. Meiner Meinung nach ist die Hauptaufgabe der Lehrer, das Lernprogramm und die Aufgaben so zu strukturieren, dass die Schüler Fortschritte machen. Das motiviert Schüler—selbst wenn das Thema nicht besonders spannend ist."

Michael Felten hat das sogar mit seiner eigenen Tochter Martina erlebt. Mit 14 Jahren
15 begann sie regelmäßig die Schule zu schwänzen. Im Unterricht langweilte sie sich zu Tode, weil sie einfach zu viele Fakten pauken musste und der Lehrplan fast nie interessant war. Es ist wichtig, dass Kinder wissen, was sie lernen, warum und in welchem Kontext das Lernmaterial steht. Wenn die Schüler im Lernprozess aktiv sind, haben sie mehr Spaß.

Martina Felten, jetzt 23 Jahre alt, weiß ganz genau, warum ihre Schuljahre so frustrierend
20 waren. „Spaß ist das Wichtigste im Klassenzimmer," meint Martina. „Die Schüler verlieren das Interesse, wenn die Lernmethoden nicht abwechslungsreich sind. Lehrer sollten den Unterricht vorsichtig planen, damit die Schüler am Ende ein Gefühl von Erfolg haben."

Die meisten Schüler wissen ganz genau, wie sie am liebsten lernen: Die Arbeit soll projektorientiert sein und eine Verbindung zu ihrem Alltagsleben haben. Fast 40% der
25 Schüler, die an der Studie teilgenommen haben, wünschen sich mehr Projektarbeit im Unterricht. Jeder fünfte Schüler meint, am besten zu lernen, wenn der Unterricht mit dem Alltag zu tun hat. Und was hat den Schülern am besten gefallen? Eine spannende Geschichte natürlich — so hat der Unterricht am meisten Spaß gemacht.

45% der Schüler finden den Unterricht unterhaltsamer, wenn sie mit Computern oder
30 Tablets lernen dürfen. In erster Linie sind es die Grundschüler, die davon begeistert sind. Diese Faszination für die digitale Welt liegt daran, dass man multimedial mit Bildern und Ton arbeitet. Dazu kommt ein weiterer Vorteil: Der Schüler kann selber entscheiden, auf welchem Niveau er arbeitet.

Ein guter Lehrer ist ständig bemüht, Interesse und Begeisterung bei seinen Schülern zu
35 wecken. Michael Felten ist keine Ausnahme — „Meine Schüler sind davon begeistert, Neues zu erfahren. Je jünger die Schüler sind, desto häufiger haben sie Erfolgserlebnisse beim Lernen. Mit zunehmendem Alter erleben die Schüler aber immer öfter demotivierende und frustrierende Situationen." Für Felten ist die Lösung klar: Er möchte mehr individuelle Ziele für Schüler sehen und er ist auch der Meinung, dass der Unterricht
40 flexibler sein sollte. Die Schüler sollten die Gelegenheit haben, ihre eigenen Interessen und Ideen einzubringen.

Aber in manchen deutschen Schulen sieht die Realität oft ganz anders aus. Erstens haben die Lehrer meist nicht genug Zeit, jede Unterrichtsstunde präzise zu planen, weil sie sehr viele andere Dinge organisieren müssen.

45 Zweitens sind nicht alle Schulen in Deutschland ausreichend mit moderner Technologie, zum Beispiel mit elektronischen Tafeln, ausgestattet.

Ein weiteres Problem für Lehrer ist, dass sich ihre Schüler im Teenager-Alter mehr für ihr Leben außerhalb der Schule interessieren.

Obwohl die Qualität des Unterrichts für den Lernerfolg entscheidend ist, sollte man den
50 Einfluss persönlicher Interessen auf Motivation und Lernbereitschaft nicht unterschätzen.

MARKS

Questions

Re-read lines 1—6.

1. What positive effect does enjoyment have on pupils' learning?   1

Re-read lines 7—13.

2. In what way do primary and secondary pupils differ in attitudes to learning?   2

3. According to Michael Felten, what is the main task of a teacher? Give **two** details.   2

Re-read lines 14—18.

4. Felten goes on to talk about his daughter's experience.

    (a) What was the first sign that Felten's daughter was unhappy at school?   1

    (b) Why was she bored in class? State **two** things.   2

Re-read lines 23—28.

5. The article then discusses learning styles.

    (a) According to statistics, in what ways do children like to learn? State **two** things.   2

    (b) What do pupils enjoy most of all?   1

Re-read lines 29—33.

6. Why do pupils in primary school like to work with digital media? State **two** things.   2

[Questions 7 to 11 are on *Page four*

MARKS

Re-read lines 34—41

7. According to Michael Felten, what is the solution to the problem of pupils' increasing lack of interest in lessons? State any **two** things.   2

Re-read lines 42—46

8. What problems do teachers face with regard to:

(a) time?   1

(b) equipment?   1

Re-read lines 47—50

9. What additional problems do teachers face?   1

10. Now consider the article as a whole.

According to the writer, what various factors are responsible for encouraging successful learning in schools? Give details from the article to justify your answer.   2

11. Translate into English:

„Spaß ist das Wichtigste . . . von Erfolg haben." (lines 20—22)   10

[END OF QUESTION PAPER]

FOR OFFICIAL USE

H

National Qualifications 2016

Mark ☐

X734/76/02

German
Directed Writing

WEDNESDAY, 1 JUNE
9:00 AM — 10:40 AM

Fill in these boxes and read what is printed below.

Full name of centre

Town

Forename(s)

Surname

Number of seat

Date of birth

Day	Month	Year	Scottish candidate number

Total marks — 10

Choose ONE scenario on *Page two* and write your answer clearly, in **German**, in the space provided in this booklet. You must clearly identify the scenario number you are attempting.

You may use a German dictionary.

Additional space for answers is provided at the end of this booklet.

Use **blue** or **black** ink.

There is a separate answer booklet for Reading. You must complete your answers for Reading in the answer booklet for Reading.

Before leaving the examination room you must give this Directed Writing question and answer booklet and your Reading Answer Booklet to the Invigilator; if you do not, you may lose all the marks for this paper.

Total marks — 10

Choose **one** of the following two scenarios.

SCENARIO 1: Culture

> Last year you and your friend went to Germany to visit your friend's German relatives.
>
> Your teacher has asked you to write, **in German**, about your experiences for your school website.

You must include the following information and **you should try to add** other relevant details:

- where you went **and** how you got there
- what the local area was like
- what you did during your stay
- whether you would recommend this experience to others

You should write approximately 120—150 words.

OR

SCENARIO 2: Employability

> Last summer you had a holiday job in Germany.
>
> On your return you were asked to write, **in German**, about your experience for the foreign language section of your school/college website.

You must include the following information and **you should try to add** other relevant details:

- what job you did **and** what it was like
- what you did during the working day
- what you did in the evenings after work
- whether you would recommend a holiday job abroad

You should write approximately 120—150 words.

ANSWER SPACE

MARKS | DO NOT WRITE IN THIS MARGIN

Scenario number

ANSWER SPACE (continued)

MARKS | DO NOT WRITE IN THIS MARGIN

ANSWER SPACE (continued)

[Turn over

MARKS DO NOT WRITE IN THIS MARGIN

ANSWER SPACE (continued)

[END OF QUESTION PAPER]

ADDITIONAL SPACE FOR ANSWERS

MARKS | DO NOT WRITE IN THIS MARGIN

MARKS | DO NOT WRITE IN THIS MARGIN

ADDITIONAL SPACE FOR ANSWERS

National Qualifications 2016

Mark

X734/76/03

German
Listening and Writing

WEDNESDAY, 1 JUNE
11:00 AM — 12:00 NOON

Fill in these boxes and read what is printed below.

Full name of centre

Town

Forename(s)

Surname

Number of seat

Date of birth

Day	Month	Year	Scottish candidate number

Total marks — 30

SECTION 1 — LISTENING — 20 marks

You will hear two items in German. **Before you hear each item, you will have one minute to study the questions.** You will hear each item twice, with an interval of one minute between playings. You will then have time to answer the questions before hearing the next item. Write your answers, in **English**, in the spaces provided.

SECTION 2 — WRITING — 10 marks

Write your answer, in **German**, in the space provided.

Attempt ALL questions. You may use a German dictionary.

Additional space for answers is provided at the end of this booklet. If you use this space you must clearly identify the question number you are attempting.

You are not allowed to leave the examination room until the end of the test.

Use **blue** or **black** ink.

Before leaving the examination room you must give this booklet to the Invigilator; if you do not, you may lose all the marks for this paper.

MARKS | DO NOT WRITE IN THIS MARGIN

SECTION 1 — LISTENING — 20 marks
Attempt ALL questions

Item 1

You listen to a German radio report about the population of cities and rural areas in Germany.

(a) A recent study has shown that more and more Germans leave small towns and villages. What evidence is there of this? State any **one** thing.   **1**

_____

(b) According to social researchers, young people are the first to move into big cities. Why is this? State any **two** things.   **2**

_____

_____

(c) Over-population can lead to problems in big cities. What are these problems? State any **two**.   **2**

_____

_____

(d) The German government wants to improve the situation in rural areas.

   (i) What help will be available? State any **one** thing.   **1**

   _____

   (ii) In what ways will these areas benefit? State any **one** thing.   **1**

   _____

(e) Consider the report as a whole. What does the report say about the situation of different areas in Germany? Tick (✓) the most appropriate box.   **1**

	Tick (✓)
Rural areas are attractive for families.	
Rural areas require significant development.	
Most people prefer life in a town to life in the countryside.	

MARKS | DO NOT WRITE IN THIS MARGIN

Item 2

Vanessa, a German teenager, has moved from the city of Berlin to a small village.

(a) Vanessa describes her new house. What does she say? State any **one** thing.

    1

_____

(b) Vanessa does not enjoy country life. Why is this? Give any **two** reasons.

    2

_____

_____

(c) Why did her parents decide to buy a house in the country? Give any **two** reasons.

    2

_____

_____

(d) Vanessa talks about her parents' jobs.

  (i) Her mother is a vet. What does Vanessa say about this? State **two** things.

    2

_____

_____

  (ii) Her father is an architect. What further information does Vanessa give about his job? State **two** things.

    2

_____

_____

(e) Vanessa still sees her friends a lot. Why is this? State any **two** things.

    2

_____

_____

(f) Vanessa concludes that she wants to move back to Berlin. What has she done to make sure this happens? State **one** thing.

    1

_____

SECTION 2 — WRITING — 10 marks

Vanessa liebt ihre Heimatstadt Berlin. Und du? Wohnst du gern in deiner Heimatstadt? Möchtest du lieber auf dem Land oder in einer Großstadt wohnen? Warum?

Schreibe 120—150 Wörter zu diesen Fragen.

_____

_____

_____

_____

_____

_____

_____

_____

_____

_____

_____

_____

_____

_____

_____

_____

_____

_____

ANSWER SPACE FOR SECTION 2 (continued)

[Turn over

MARKS | DO NOT WRITE IN THIS MARGIN

ANSWER SPACE FOR SECTION 2 (continued)

[END OF QUESTION PAPER]

MARKS | DO NOT WRITE IN THIS MARGIN

ADDITIONAL SPACE FOR ANSWERS

Page seven

ADDITIONAL SPACE FOR ANSWERS

National Qualifications 2016

X734/76/13

German
Listening Transcript

WEDNESDAY, 1 JUNE

11:00 AM — 12:00 NOON

This paper must not be seen by any candidate.

The material overleaf is provided for use in an emergency only (eg the recording or equipment proving faulty) or where permission has been given in advance by SQA for the material to be read to candidates with additional support needs. The material must be read exactly as printed.

Instructions to reader(s):

For each item, read the English **once**, then read the German **twice**, with an interval of 1 minute between the two readings. On completion of the second reading of Item Number One, pause for the length of time indicated in brackets after the item, to allow the candidates to write their answers.

Where special arrangements have been agreed in advance to allow the reading of the material, those sections marked **(f)** should be read by a female speaker and those marked **(m)** by a male; those sections marked **(t)** should be read by the teacher.

(t)   **Item Number One**

You listen to a German radio report about the population of cities and rural areas in Germany.

You now have one minute to study the questions for Item Number One.

(m/f)   Laut einer Studie verlassen immer mehr Deutsche die Kleinstädte und Dörfer auf dem Land. Im Moment wohnen 17 Prozent der Deutschen in einer Großstadt. Im Jahr 2030 werden es sogar 19 Prozent sein. In den nächsten Jahren werden 12 Millionen Deutsche vom Land in die Stadt ziehen.

Sozialwissenschaftler warnen vor diesem Trend, weil es in erster Linie junge Menschen sind, die in die Großstädte gehen. Dort finden sie einerseits bessere Arbeitsmöglichkeiten und Karrierechancen und andererseits können sie in der Stadt ihre Freizeit interessanter verbringen, denn es gibt Kinos, Diskos, Restaurants, Clubs und Sportvereine — auf dem Land ist so ein kulturelles Angebot selten.

Außerdem kann es Probleme geben, wenn immer mehr Menschen in Großstädten wohnen: Wohnungen und Häuser sind teuer, zu viele Autos behindern den Verkehr besonders in der Stadtmitte. Es gibt nicht genug Kindergärten und in den Schulen gehen oft mehr als 30 Schüler in eine Klasse.

Die Bundesregierung hat ein Programm aufgestellt, um diese Entwicklung zu stoppen. Jedes Jahr gibt Deutschland 10 Millionen Euro aus, damit das Leben auf dem Land wieder attraktiver wird.

Mit dem Geld soll die Lebensqualität in den Dörfern verbessert werden — dazu gehört nicht nur Hilfe für Bauern und landwirtschaftliche Betriebe. Mehr öffentliche Transportmittel, mehr Supermärkte und vor allem eine schnellere Internetverbindung stehen ganz oben auf der Liste der Verbesserungen.

Außerdem sollen Schulen und Jobcenter junge Leute über Berufschancen auf dem Land informieren und bei der Bewerbung unterstützen. Nur wenn junge Leute auf dem Land eine interessante Perspektive haben, kann eine weitere Abwanderung in große Städte verhindert werden.

(2 minutes)

(t)   **Item Number Two**

Vanessa, a German teenager, has moved from the city of Berlin to a small village.

You now have one minute to study the questions for Item Number Two.

(m)   Hallo, Vanessa. Wie gefällt es dir in deinem neuen Haus?

(f)   Ja, hallo. Naja, das Haus ist schon okay — in Berlin haben wir einer Wohnung im dritten Stock gewohnt, hier haben wir ein großes Haus mit Garten. Ich habe mein eigenes Zimmer und muss nicht mit meiner Schwester zusammen wohnen und meine Eltern haben gesagt, wir können sogar einen Hund haben.

(m)   Das ist doch schön. Und wie findest du das Leben auf dem Land?

(f)   Es gefällt mir überhaupt nicht! Ich liebe die Großstadt — und ganz besonders Berlin. Hier auf dem Land ist es viel zu ruhig und jeden Tag riecht es nach Kuhstall, sodass ich mein Fenster nicht öffnen kann!

(m)   Naja, das ist eben die Landluft! Warum haben deine Eltern denn überhaupt ein Haus auf dem Land gekauft?

(f)   Meine Mutter findet das Leben in der Großstadt sehr anstrengend. Sie hat Probleme mit den vielen Autos und den vielen Menschen auf der Straße und findet, dass es jeden Tag ziemlich laut und schmutzig ist. Tja, und mein Vater kommt aus einem kleinen Dorf und möchte lieber auf dem Land als in der Stadt leben.

(m)   Und wie ist das mit Arbeit für deine Eltern?

(f)   Also, meine Mutter ist Tierärztin — für sie ist das Landleben ideal, weil es hier mehr als genug Arbeit gibt. Sie freut sich schon auf die vielen Pferde, Kühe, Schafe und Schweine, denn solche großen Tiere hat sie in Berlin sehr selten behandelt. Und mein Vater arbeitet von zu Hause — er ist Architekt und hat sein Büro im Keller. Er liebt die Ruhe auf dem Land, weil er sich dann besser konzentrieren kann.

(m)   Deine Freunde sind sicher alle in Berlin. Siehst du sie oft?

(f)   Ja, das ist zum Glück kein Problem. Wir wohnen nur 10 Kilometer weg von Berlin, sodass ich auch die Schule nicht wechseln muss und jeden Tag mit dem Bus zum Gymnasium fahre. Am Wochenende besuche ich normalerweise meine beste Freundin und darf bei ihr übernachten — meine Eltern sind in dieser Hinsicht modern und vertrauen mir. Ohne Kontakt zu meinen Freunden würde ich das Landleben noch schwieriger finden.

(m)   Und wenn du mit der Schule fertig bist, wo wirst du dann wohnen?

(f)   Na in Berlin! Das ist doch klar. Ich mache in diesem Jahr mein Abitur und habe mich schon an allen vier Berliner Universitäten beworben. Wenn ich einen Studienplatz bekomme, werde ich sofort eine kleine Wohnung suchen und umziehen. Am liebsten würde ich mit meiner besten Freundin zusammen wohnen. Das Landleben ist bestimmt attraktiv für Familien mit kleinen Kindern und für ältere Leute — aber nicht für Jugendliche und überhaupt nicht für mich!

(m)   Naja, Berlin ist eben Berlin. Viel Glück bei der Wohnungssuche.

(t)   **End of recording.**

[END OF TRANSCRIPT]

Page three

[BLANK PAGE]

DO NOT WRITE ON THIS PAGE

HIGHER

2017

National Qualifications 2017

X734/76/11

German Reading

FRIDAY, 2 JUNE
9:00 AM – 10:40 AM

Total marks — 30

Attempt ALL questions.

Write your answers clearly, in **English**, in the Reading answer booklet provided. In the answer booklet you must clearly identify the question number you are attempting.

You may use a German dictionary.

Use **blue** or **black** ink.

There is a separate question and answer booklet for Directed Writing. You must complete your answer for Directed Writing in the question and answer booklet for Directed Writing.

Before leaving the examination room you must give your Reading answer booklet and your Directed Writing question and answer booklet to the Invigilator; if you do not, you may lose all the marks for this paper.

Total marks — 30

Attempt ALL questions

Read the whole article carefully and then answer, in **English**, ALL the questions that follow.

In this article, the writer discusses holidays without parents.

Ferien ohne Eltern — Gewinn oder Verlust?

Ferien ohne Eltern werden immer beliebter. In der Bundesrepublik Deutschland machen jedes Jahr etwa 1,7 Millionen Kinder und Jugendliche ohne ihre Eltern Ferien. Der Markt für Jugendreisen aller Art im Inland und Ausland expandiert ständig und hat sich in den letzten fünf Jahren verdoppelt.

5   Die Gründe dafür sind unterschiedlich: Während die Eltern sich einen ruhigen und erholsamen Urlaub wünschen, wollen ihre Kinder Spaß haben und etwas Spannendes erleben. Ein Besuch in einem Museum oder eine Stadtrundfahrt in einer europäischen Metropole kann Eltern begeistern, aber Kinder und Jugendliche langweilen. In einem Familienurlaub ist es oftmals schwierig, allen Erwartungen gerecht zu werden.

10 Wenn Kinder ohne ihre Eltern Ferien machen wollen, sollten die Eltern einen Reiseanbieter suchen, der auf Jugendreisen spezialisiert ist. Dort finden sie Hilfe und Unterstützung, damit die geplanten Ferien ein Erfolg werden. Außerdem sollten sich die Eltern die Frage stellen, ob ihr Kind wirklich reif genug ist, um alleine oder in einer Gruppe verreisen zu können. Man sollte auch bedenken, dass es verschiedene Arten von Jugendreisen gibt und in einem

15 Gespräch mit dem Kind herausfinden, ob ein Skiurlaub in Frankreich, eine Sprachreise nach England oder ein Feriencamp an der Ostsee die richtige Wahl ist.

Marita Sammers arbeitet seit zehn Jahren als Reiseleiterin für Jugendreisen. Sie bereitet jede Reise gründlich vor. „Zuerst muss ich herausfinden, was genau die Eltern und ihre Kinder von der Reise erwarten. Weiterhin muss ich wissen, wie viel Geld die Eltern für die Jugendreise

20 ausgeben können, damit es keine Probleme mit dem Familienbudget gibt. Jedoch sind für mich die möglichen Ängste und Sorgen der Eltern das Allerwichtigste. Sie haben ihr Kind seit der Geburt immer in ihrer Nähe gehabt — und plötzlich möchte ihr Sohn oder ihre Tochter mit einer Jugendgruppe Ferien machen. Das ist für viele Eltern ein größeres Problem, als man vielleicht denkt."

25 Trotz elterlicher Emotionen — Jugendreisen ohne Eltern boomen in Deutschland, denn die Vorteile liegen auf der Hand. Es geht nicht nur um individuelle Ferien, damit jeder seinen Interessen nachgehen kann. Kinder und Jugendliche lernen bei Jugendreisen, in einer Gruppe zu leben und zu kooperieren. Sie sind mit Gleichaltrigen zusammen und haben in einem betreuten Umfeld die Chance, sich frei zu entwickeln, neue Freunde zu finden und

30 großartige Dinge zu erleben.

<u>Zu Hause in vertrauter Umgebung treffen die Eltern oft Entscheidungen für ihre Kinder. Wenn Kinder ohne ihre Eltern in ein Feriencamp fahren, müssen sie selbst Verantwortung tragen. In vielen Fällen macht diese Erfahrung Jugendliche stärker und selbstbewusster.</u>

Tilo Tautz (16 Jahre alt) war im letzten Jahr mit einer Jugendgruppe und ohne seine Eltern

35 unterwegs. Er hat zwei Wochen in einem Feriencamp an der Ostsee verbracht und berichtet von seinen Erfahrungen: „Im Camp habe ich Dinge gelernt und erlebt, die ich in meinem Alltag in Berlin nicht erleben kann: einen Sonnenaufgang morgens am Meer, am Strand schlafen und mit anderen Jugendlichen abends am Lagerfeuer sitzen. Ich habe sehr viele neue Leute kennen gelernt und diese Erfahrung hat mich ermutigt, im nächsten Jahr mit

40 einer Jugendgruppe ins Ausland zu fahren. Dann möchte ich Abenteuerferien in Norwegen machen."

Gab es auch schwierige Momente für Tilo? „Ja, doch, das kann man schon sagen. In den ersten Tagen hat meine Mutter mich ständig auf dem Handy angerufen und mindestens zehn SMS geschickt. Das war mir peinlich. Naja, und meine Familie hat mir ein bisschen gefehlt.
45 Doch ein Mädchen aus meiner Gruppe hatte sogar Heimweh nach ihrem Pferd! Aber unsere Teamer — das sind die Betreuer in einem Jugendcamp — haben sehr gut reagiert. Sie haben sich sehr um das Mädchen gekümmert und für den nächsten Tag einen Ausflug zu einem Reitzentrum organisiert."

Eine Reise ohne Eltern ist für Kinder und Jugendliche eine echte Chance, etwas ganz Neues
50 zu erleben und neue Seiten an sich kennen zu lernen. Die meisten Jugendlichen gehen gestärkt aus dieser Erfahrung heraus und haben viele schöne Erinnerungen an die ersten Ferien ohne Eltern.

MARKS

Questions

Re-read lines 1—4.

1. Holidays without parents are becoming more and more popular with young Germans. What evidence is there for this? State any **two** things.   2

Re-read lines 5—9.

2. Why do parents and children decide to spend their holidays separately? State **three** things.   3

Re-read lines 10—16.

3. What should parents do if their children want to go on holiday without them? State **three** things.   3

Re-read lines 17—24.

4. Marita Sammers is a travel agent for young people.

   (a) She prepares every trip carefully. What does she have to find out first? State any **one** thing.   1

   (b) According to Marita, what is the most important thing to consider? Give **one** detail.   1

Re-read lines 25—30.

5. According to the article, what are the advantages of holidays without parents? State **three** things.   3

MARKS

Re-read lines 34—48.

6. Tilo Tautz spent his holiday last year without his parents.

    (a) In what way was this a good experience for him? Give **three** details.   3

    (b) What kind of difficulties did Tilo experience? State **two** things.   2

Now consider the article as a whole.

7. Is going on holiday without parents a valuable experience? Give reasons for your answer with reference to the text.   2

8. Translate into English:

    „Zu Hause in vertrauter Umgebung . . . stärker und selbstbewusster." (lines 31 to 33)   10

[END OF QUESTION PAPER]

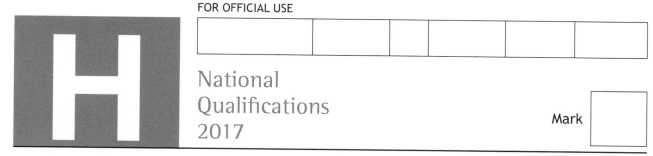

National Qualifications 2017

Mark

X734/76/02

**German
Directed Writing**

FRIDAY, 2 JUNE
9:00 AM — 10:40 AM

Fill in these boxes and read what is printed below.

Full name of centre

Town

Forename(s)

Surname

Number of seat

Date of birth

Day	Month	Year	Scottish candidate number

Total marks — 10

Choose ONE scenario on *Page two* and write your answer clearly, in **German**, in the space provided in this booklet. You must clearly identify the scenario number you are attempting.

You may use a German dictionary.

Additional space for answers is provided at the end of this booklet.

Use **blue** or **black** ink.

There is a separate answer booklet for Reading. You must complete your answers for Reading in the answer booklet for Reading.

Before leaving the examination room you must give this Directed Writing question and answer booklet and your Reading answer booklet to the Invigilator; if you do not, you may lose all the marks for this paper.

Total marks — 10

Choose **one** from the following two scenarios.

Scenario 1: Learning

> You have just come back from Germany where you spent two weeks as an exchange student in your German partner school/college. You have been asked to write a report in **German** for the school website.

You must include the following information and **you should try to add** other relevant details:

- how you travelled **and** what the journey was like
- what you did during the school day
- how you spent your spare time
- whether you plan to repeat the experience

You should write approximately 120—150 words.

OR

Scenario 2: Employability

> Last summer you worked at a hotel in Germany. You have been asked to write a report in **German** about your trip for your school/college magazine.

You must include the following information and **you should try to add** other relevant details:

- how you travelled **and** what you did during the journey
- what your duties were in the hotel
- how you spent your free time in the evenings
- whether you would recommend working in Germany

You should write approximately 120—150 words.

MARKS | DO NOT WRITE IN THIS MARGIN

ANSWER SPACE

Scenario number [   ]

_____

_____

_____

_____

_____

_____

_____

_____

_____

_____

_____

_____

_____

_____

_____

_____

_____

_____

_____

_____

_____

_____

_____

_____

_____

MARKS | DO NOT WRITE IN THIS MARGIN

ANSWER SPACE (continued)

MARKS | DO NOT WRITE IN THIS MARGIN

ANSWER SPACE (continued)

ANSWER SPACE (continued)

[END OF QUESTION PAPER]

ADDITIONAL SPACE FOR ANSWERS

MARKS | DO NOT WRITE IN THIS MARGIN

MARKS | DO NOT WRITE IN THIS MARGIN

ADDITIONAL SPACE FOR ANSWERS

National
Qualifications
2017

Mark

X734/76/03

German
Listening and Writing

FRIDAY, 2 JUNE
11:00 AM — 12:00 NOON

Fill in these boxes and read what is printed below.

Full name of centre

Town

Forename(s)

Surname

Number of seat

Date of birth

Day	Month	Year	Scottish candidate number

Total marks — 30

SECTION 1 — LISTENING — 20 marks

You will hear two items in German. **Before you hear each item, you will have one minute to study the questions.** You will hear each item twice, with an interval of one minute between playings. You will then have time to answer the questions before hearing the next item. Write your answers clearly, in **English**, in the spaces provided.

SECTION 2 — WRITING — 10 marks

Write your answer clearly, in **German**, in the space provided.

You may use a German dictionary.

Additional space for answers is provided at the end of this booklet. If you use this space you must clearly identify the question number you are attempting.

Use **blue** or **black** ink.

You are not allowed to leave the examination room until the end of the test.

Before leaving the examination room you must give this booklet to the Invigilator; if you do not, you may lose all the marks for this paper.

MARKS | DO NOT WRITE IN THIS MARGIN

SECTION 1 — LISTENING — 20 marks

Attempt ALL questions

Item 1

You listen to a German radio report about recent developments in the population of Germany.

(a) A recent survey has shown that Germany's population is aging. What will the situation be in 2030? State **one** thing.   **1**

_____

_____

(b) According to experts, what are the reasons for this trend? State **three** things.   **3**

_____

_____

_____

_____

(c) Germany needs to be prepared for the effects of its aging population. In what way do experts anticipate changes in:

   (i) The housing situation?   **1**

_____

   (ii) The job market?   **1**

_____

(d) According to the report, what advantages does membership of the European Union bring to Germany? State any **two** things.   **2**

_____

_____

_____

MARKS | DO NOT WRITE IN THIS MARGIN

Item 2

Robert, a German student, is being interviewed about his life in a new multi-generational housing concept.

(a) Robert describes the house he lives in. What does he say? Give any **two** details.

2

_____

_____

(b) Older and younger people live close together. What **else** is special about this type of house? State **two** things.

2

_____

_____

_____

(c) What is the basic rule in this house?

1

_____

_____

_____

(d) Robert talks about the advantages of living here.

  (i) What are the advantages? State any **two** things.

2

_____

_____

_____

  (ii) There have to be compromises however. State any **two**.

2

_____

_____

_____

MARKS | DO NOT WRITE IN THIS MARGIN

Item 2 (continued)

(e) Robert's elderly neighbours help him when he is away. What do they do for him? State any **one** thing.

1

_____

_____

(f) Why did Robert really want to live in the multi-generational house? Give **two** reasons.

2

_____

_____

_____

SECTION 2 — WRITING — 10 marks

Robert wohnt mit älteren Menschen in einem Haus. Und du? Mit welchen Personen wohnst du zusammen? Kommst du gut mit ihnen aus? Warum? Warum nicht?

Schreibe 120—150 Wörter zu diesen Fragen.

[Turn over

ANSWER SPACE FOR SECTION 2 (continued)

MARKS | DO NOT WRITE IN THIS MARGIN

ANSWER SPACE FOR SECTION 2 (continued)

[END OF QUESTION PAPER]

MARKS | DO NOT WRITE IN THIS MARGIN

ADDITIONAL SPACE FOR ANSWERS

MARKS | DO NOT WRITE IN THIS MARGIN

ADDITIONAL SPACE FOR ANSWERS

[BLANK PAGE]

DO NOT WRITE ON THIS PAGE

National Qualifications 2017

X734/76/13

German
Listening Transcript

FRIDAY, 2 JUNE

11:00 AM — 12:00 NOON

This paper must not be seen by any candidate.

The material overleaf is provided for use in an emergency only (eg the recording or equipment proving faulty) or where permission has been given in advance by SQA for the material to be read to candidates with additional support needs. The material must be read exactly as printed.

Instructions to reader(s):

For each item, read the English **once**, then read the German **twice**, with an interval of 1 minute between the two readings. On completion of the second reading of Item Number One, pause for the length of time indicated in brackets after the item, to allow the candidates to write their answers.

Where special arrangements have been agreed in advance to allow the reading of the material, those sections marked **(f)** should be read by a female speaker and those marked **(m)** by a male; those sections marked **(t)** should be read by the teacher.

(t) **Item Number One**

You listen to a German radio report about recent developments in the population of Germany.

You now have one minute to study the questions for Item Number One.

(m/f) Laut einer Studie der Bundesregierung wird es in der Zukunft immer mehr ältere Menschen in Deutschland geben. Im Jahr 2030 werden 70% der Deutschen älter als 30 Jahre sein.

Experten sehen mehrere Gründe für diesen dramatischen Trend: In Deutschland werden immer weniger Kinder geboren, weil die meisten Familien nur ein oder maximal zwei Kinder haben. Außerdem ist eine gesunde Lebensweise für viele Deutsche sehr wichtig. Weiterhin helfen moderne Medizin und neue Medikamente, Krankheiten besser zu behandeln, sodass viele Menschen immer älter werden.

Es ist notwendig, dass Deutschland auf seine älter werdende Bevölkerung vorbereitet ist. Mehr Wohnungen, die speziell für ältere Menschen geeignet sind, müssen gebaut werden.

Außerdem wird Deutschland in der Zukunft mehr Krankenschwestern und Sozialarbeiter brauchen. Wenn man dieses Personal nicht im Land findet, muss man im Ausland suchen.

Die Europäische Union ist ein ideales Modell für den Arbeitsmarkt der Zukunft in Deutschland, denn die Europäer haben das Recht in jedem Land der EU zu leben und zu arbeiten. Somit kann es für alle Länder in Europa leichter sein, die Probleme der Gegenwart und der Zukunft gemeinsam zu lösen.

(2 minutes)

(t)   **Item Number Two**

Robert, a German student, is being interviewed about his life in a new multi-generational housing concept.

You now have one minute to study the questions for Item Number Two.

(f)   Hallo Robert, du wohnst in einem Mehr-Generationen-Haus. Kannst du uns etwas über dieses Haus erzählen?

(m)   Ja, hallo, also . . . ich wohne seit sechs Monaten in einem Haus in der Stadtmitte. Das Haus ist relativ groß und hat einen wunderbaren Garten mit Bänken und vielen Bäumen.

(f)   Das ist ja toll. Aber sag mal, was ist das Besondere an diesem Haus?

(m)   Naja, das Besondere ist, dass ältere und jüngere Menschen zusammen in diesem Haus wohnen. Außerdem gibt es ein gemeinsames Freizeitzimmer, wo wir uns regelmäßig treffen. Dann spielen wir Karten — oder sogar Videospiele. Und jede Woche oganisieren wir einen Einkaufstag und fahren gemeinsam mit dem Bus zum Supermarkt!

(f)   Aber warum habt ihr ein Freizeitzimmer? Es gibt doch Wohnungen im Haus . . .

(m)   Das Freizeitzimmer ist ein neutraler Raum, wo jeder kommen und gehen kann, wie er gerne möchte. Das ist eine Grundregel in unserem Haus: Alles ist freiwillig und niemand muss etwas machen, wenn er das nicht will.

(f)   Welche Vorteile hat dieses Wohnkonzept für dich?

(m)   Hmmm . . . ich denke, dass ich sehr viel von meinen älteren Nachbarn lernen kann, und wenn ich ein Problem habe, kann ich sie fragen. Ein anderer Vorteil ist auch, dass die älteren Menschen nicht alleine leben müssen und dass die jüngeren Nachbarn für sie da sind.

(f)   Gibt es auch Nachteile für dich?

(m)   Nein, das kann ich nicht sagen. Aber man muss schon Kompromisse eingehen. In erster Linie sollte man nicht zu laut sein. Wenn man Musik hören will, sollte man den Kopfhörer benutzen und wilde Partys muss man in der Disko feiern und nicht zu Hause. Aber das sind doch Kleinigkeiten.

(f)   Haben deine älteren Nachbarn dir auch schon mal geholfen?

(m)   Oh ja, sehr oft. Wenn ich nicht zu Hause bin, nehmen sie die Post aus dem Kasten, sie gießen die Blumen und füttern meine Katze. Da muss ich mir keine Sorgen machen.

(f)   Und warum wolltest du unbedingt in einem Mehr-Generationen-Haus wohnen?

(m)   Naja, erstens wollte ich meine eigene Wohnung in der Stadtmitte haben. Das hat gut funktioniert. Und zweitens bin ich nicht gern alleine. Ich bin ein sozialer Typ, der gern mit Menschen zu tun hat. Außerdem finde ich, dass das Älterwerden ein normaler Prozess ist, den man nicht stoppen kann.

(f)   Vielen Dank, Robert. Das war ein gutes Schlusswort.

(t)   **End of recording.**

[END OF TRANSCRIPT]

Page three

[BLANK PAGE]

DO NOT WRITE ON THIS PAGE

HIGHER

2018

National Qualifications 2018

X734/76/11

German Reading

MONDAY, 4 JUNE
9:00 AM — 10:40 AM

Total marks — 30

Attempt ALL questions.

Write your answers clearly, in **English**, in the Reading answer booklet provided. In the answer booklet you must clearly identify the question number you are attempting.

You may use a German dictionary.

Use **blue** or **black** ink.

There is a separate question and answer booklet for Directed Writing. You must complete your answer for Directed Writing in the question and answer booklet for Directed Writing.

Before leaving the examination room you must give your Reading answer booklet and your Directed Writing question and answer booklet to the Invigilator; if you do not, you may lose all the marks for this paper.

Total marks — 30

Attempt ALL questions

Read the whole article carefully and then answer, in **English**, ALL the questions that follow.

This article discusses the experiences of young Spanish people working in Germany.

Spanische Sonne — oder eine Karriere in Deutschland?

Jedes Jahr verlassen immer mehr junge Spanier ihre Heimat. Viele von ihnen kommen nach Deutschland, weil mehr als die Hälfte der jungen Spanier zwischen 15 und 24 keine Arbeit in ihrem Heimatland Spanien haben. In Deutschland angekommen, stellt sich die Frage: Heimweh oder Arbeitslosigkeit — was ist schlimmer?

5 Seit Juni letzten Jahres lebt Miguel Abello in Heidelberg. Dort macht er eine Ausbildung bei einer Baufirma, obwohl er in seiner Heimat Spanien schon fast fünf Jahre lang als Maurer gearbeitet hat. Doch Miguel hatte in Spanien nie einen festen Arbeitsvertrag. Dann wurde er arbeitslos. Das Essen seiner Mutter ist das Einzige, was Miguel Abello in Deutschland so richtig vermisst. „Ich habe kein Heimweh nach Spanien und deshalb denke ich noch nicht
10 daran zurückzukehren. Außerdem habe ich im Moment in Deutschland beruflich bessere Chancen. In Spanien würde ich wahrscheinlich wieder arbeitslos sein und meine Familie müsste mich finanziell unterstützen", sagt der 26-Jährige.

Momentan leben mehr als 100.000 Spanier in Deutschland. Viele von ihnen machen — wie Miguel — eine Ausbildung, weil es in Deutschland einen Mangel an Facharbeitern gibt.
15 Spanische Arbeitskräfte werden besonders in praktischen Berufen, im Bereich Altenpflege und in der Gastronomie gebraucht, weil sie normalerweise bereits Erfahrung mitbringen und mindestens zwei Fremdsprachen sprechen.

Laura Fuentes profitiert ebenfalls von dem Interesse der deutschen Unternehmen an ausländischen Fachkräften: Sie arbeitet mit Miguel Abello im gleichen Betrieb in Heidelberg.
20 Die beiden Spanier haben den gleichen Intensivsprachkurs für Deutsch in Spanien gemacht, jetzt wohnen sie in Heidelberg in der gleichen Straße. „Wir sprechen viel Spanisch zusammen, aber unser Deutsch wird besser", erzählt die 25-Jährige.

„Am Anfang hatte ich große Schwierigkeiten mit der deutschen Sprache, obwohl meine Kollegen sehr hilfsbereit und verständnisvoll waren. Viele Deutsche sprechen mit einem
25 starken Akzent, der für mich schwierig zu verstehen war. Außerdem musste ich die Grammatik gründlich studieren." Aber jetzt ist das alles kein Problem mehr für sie — Laura ist im Moment glücklich in Heidelberg, obwohl sie ihre spanische Basketballmannschaft vermisst.

Dennoch wird sie nachdenklich, als sie von ihrer Heimat erzählt. Die junge Spanierin kommt
30 aus Sevilla, wo sie eine Ausbildung gemacht hat. „Man findet Arbeit in Spanien, aber das Problem ist, dass man von der Bezahlung nicht leben kann", erzählt sie. Die Firma in Heidelberg hat ihr eine Chance und eine Perspektive gegeben. „Ich hatte Glück, aber ewig werde ich hier nicht bleiben." Zu sehr fehlten die vertraute Sprache, die spanische Küche sowie die typisch spanischen Feste mit Freunden und Familie.

35 Für die deutschen Arbeitgeber ist der Wunsch der spanischen Mitarbeiter, ins Heimatland zurückzukehren, die größte Herausforderung. Jutta Hoffmann ist Projektleiterin in einem Arbeitsamt in Hamburg. Sie unterstützt spanische Arbeitskräfte bei der Integration in Deutschland. „Bislang sind die meisten der spanischen Arbeiter nicht länger als sieben Jahre in Deutschland geblieben. Viele junge Spanier gehen zurück, weil sie ihre eigene Familie in
40 Spanien gründen wollen oder weil der Freund oder die Freundin nicht nach Deutschland kommen will."

Deutsche Betriebe brauchen die jungen Ausländer immer noch. Deshalb haben viele Arbeitgeber Anreize geschaffen, um die Mitarbeiter zu überzeugen in Deutschland zu bleiben. Sie unterstützen ausländische Mitarbeiter bei der Suche nach einer passenden
45 Wohnung. Die meisten Firmen bieten nach einer Probezeit von drei Monaten einen Firmenwagen, den man auch privat nutzen kann. Außerdem stellen die Arbeitgeber sicher, dass die jährliche Lohnerhöhung pünktlich gezahlt wird. Manchmal finanzieren Firmen sogar den Jahresurlaub ihrer spanischen Mitarbeiter, damit sie ihre Familie in Spanien besuchen können.

50 Nach ihrem letzten Besuch in Spanien und nach vielen Gesprächen mit Familie und Freunden sind Miguel und Laura immer noch skeptisch hinsichtlich einer Zukunft in ihrer Heimat. „Kein Wunder, dass so viele junge Leute gehen wollen, denn die Situation in Spanien hat sich noch nicht geändert", sagen die beiden. „Die Tatsache, dass so viele Leute unser Land verlassen, nennen wir auf Spanisch *fuga de cerebros*' — das heißt auf Deutsch ‚die Flucht der Gehirne'.
55 Ob die Bezeichnung passt, können wir nicht beurteilen. Wir sind gegangen, weil wir Leute sind, die arbeiten wollen."

MARKS

Questions

Re-read lines 1—4.

1. Why do many young people leave Spain and come to Germany?   1

Re-read lines 5—12.

2. Miguel Abello has come to Germany from Spain.

    (a) What brought Miguel to Heidelberg? Give any **two** details.   2

    (b) Why is he not thinking about returning to Spain yet? State any **two** things.   2

Re-read lines 13—17.

3. More than 100,000 Spanish people live in Germany.

    (a) Why do so many young Spanish people do an apprenticeship in Germany?   1

    (b) Spanish workers are in demand in some industries. Why is this? State **two** things.   2

Re-read lines 18—22.

4. Laura Fuentes is also Spanish and living in Heidelberg.

    What else do Laura and Miguel have in common? Give **three** details.   3

MARKS

Questions (continued)

Re-read lines 29–34.

5. Laura goes on to say more about her life in Germany.

    (a) What is the problem with working in Spain?   1

    (b) Why does she think she won't stay in Germany forever? Give any **two** details.   2

Re-read lines 35–41.

6. According to Jutta Hoffmann, what are the main reasons that Spanish workers return
    to Spain? State any **one** thing.   1

Re-read lines 42–49.

7. What do German employers do to encourage young foreign workers to stay in
    Germany? Give any **two** details.   2

Re-read lines 50–56.

8. Many young people are still leaving Spain. Why is this the case, according to Miguel
    and Laura?   1

Now consider the article as a whole.

9. Does the article present a positive or negative impression of employment for young
    Spanish people in Germany? Give details from the text to justify your answer.   2

10. Translate into English:

    „Am Anfang hatte ich . . . gründlich studieren." (lines 23–26)   10

[END OF QUESTION PAPER]

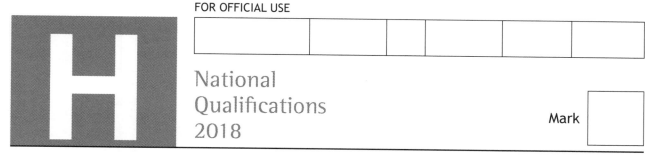

H

National Qualifications 2018

Mark

X734/76/02

German
Directed Writing

MONDAY, 4 JUNE

9:00 AM — 10:40 AM

Fill in these boxes and read what is printed below.

Full name of centre

Town

Forename(s)

Surname

Number of seat

Date of birth

Day	Month	Year	Scottish candidate number

Total marks — 10

Choose ONE scenario on *Page two* and write your answer clearly, in **German**, in the space provided in this booklet. You must clearly identify the scenario number you are attempting.

You may use a German dictionary.

Additional space for answers is provided at the end of this booklet.

Use **blue** or **black** ink.

There is a separate answer booklet for Reading. You must complete your answers for Reading in the answer booklet for Reading.

Before leaving the examination room you must give this Directed Writing question and answer booklet and your Reading answer booklet to the Invigilator; if you do not, you may lose all the marks for this paper.

Total marks — 10

Choose **one** from the following two scenarios.

Scenario 1: Society

> Last summer you and your family went on holiday to a German-speaking country. Your school/college has asked you to write about your time there in **German** for the language section of your school/college website.

You must include the following information and **you should try to add** other relevant details:

- where exactly you went **and** what the journey was like
- how well you got on with your family
- what you did during your stay
- whether or not you would recommend going on holiday with family

You should write approximately 120—150 words.

OR

Scenario 2: Culture

> While on holiday in a German-speaking country, you went to a music festival. You write about your experience in **German** for the language section of your school/college website.

You must include the following information and **you should try to add** other relevant details:

- what the journey was like **and** where you stayed
- what you enjoyed about the festival
- what else you did during your stay
- whether or not you would consider going to a similar event again

You should write approximately 120—150 words.

MARKS | DO NOT WRITE IN THIS MARGIN

ANSWER SPACE

Scenario number

_____

_____

_____

_____

_____

_____

_____

_____

_____

_____

_____

_____

_____

_____

_____

_____

_____

_____

_____

_____

_____

_____

_____

_____

_____

MARKS | DO NOT WRITE IN THIS MARGIN

ANSWER SPACE (continued)

ANSWER SPACE (continued)

[Turn over

MARKS | DO NOT WRITE IN THIS MARGIN

ANSWER SPACE (continued)

[END OF QUESTION PAPER]

MARKS | DO NOT WRITE IN THIS MARGIN

ADDITIONAL SPACE FOR ANSWERS

ADDITIONAL SPACE FOR ANSWERS

National Qualifications 2018

Mark

X734/76/03

German
Listening and Writing

MONDAY, 4 JUNE
11:00 AM — 12:00 NOON

Fill in these boxes and read what is printed below.

Full name of centre

Town

Forename(s)

Surname

Number of seat

Date of birth

Day	Month	Year	Scottish candidate number

Total marks — 30

SECTION 1 — LISTENING — 20 marks

You will hear two items in German. **Before you hear each item, you will have one minute to study the questions.** You will hear each item twice, with an interval of one minute between playings. You will then have time to answer the questions before hearing the next item. Write your answers clearly, in **English**, in the spaces provided.

SECTION 2 — WRITING — 10 marks

Write your answer clearly, in **German**, in the space provided.

You may use a German dictionary.

Additional space for answers is provided at the end of this booklet. If you use this space you must clearly identify the question number you are attempting.

Use **blue** or **black** ink.

You are not allowed to leave the examination room until the end of the test.

Before leaving the examination room you must give this booklet to the Invigilator; if you do not, you may lose all the marks for this paper.

MARKS | DO NOT WRITE IN THIS MARGIN

SECTION 1 — LISTENING — 20 marks
Attempt ALL questions

Item 1

You listen to Sebastian talking on the radio about his school, which specialises in sport.

(a) What did Sebastian have to do to get his place at the sports school? State **two** things.   **2**

_____

_____

(b) Sebastian tells us that life in the sports school is demanding. Give any **three** details.   **3**

_____

_____

(c) What does Sebastian say about his teachers? State any **one** thing.   **1**

_____

_____

(d) Apart from sport, what other things do pupils learn? State any **one** thing.   **1**

_____

_____

(e) What does Sebastian like best about his school? State any **one** thing.   **1**

_____

_____

MARKS | DO NOT WRITE IN THIS MARGIN

Item 2

Sebastian and his mother talk about school life at a boarding school.

(a) Why did Sebastian's mother go to boarding school? State **two** things.

2

_____

_____

(b) What was life like for her at boarding school? State any **two** things.

2

_____

_____

(c) When did she see her parents? Give any **two** details.

2

_____

_____

(d) What was her school day like? Give any **two** details.

2

_____

_____

(e) What does she say about her experience of learning languages? Give any **two** details.

2

_____

_____

(f) Sebastian's mother says that boarding schools are not better than other schools. What does she say? State **two** things.

2

_____

_____

[Turn over

MARKS | DO NOT WRITE IN THIS MARGIN

SECTION 2 — WRITING — 10 marks

Sebastian geht in eine Sportschule. In was für eine Schule gehst du? Wie findest du deinen Schulalltag? Gefällt dir deine Schule? Warum? Warum nicht?

Schreibe 120—150 Wörter zu diesen Fragen.

_____

_____

_____

_____

_____

_____

_____

_____

_____

_____

_____

_____

_____

_____

_____

_____

_____

MARKS | DO NOT WRITE IN THIS MARGIN

ANSWER SPACE FOR SECTION 2 (continued)

MARKS | DO NOT WRITE IN THIS MARGIN

ANSWER SPACE FOR SECTION 2 (continued)

[END OF QUESTION PAPER]

MARKS | DO NOT WRITE IN THIS MARGIN

ADDITIONAL SPACE FOR ANSWERS

ADDITIONAL SPACE FOR ANSWERS

National
Qualifications
2018

X734/76/13

German
Listening Transcript

MONDAY, 4 JUNE

11:00 AM — 12:00 NOON

This paper must not be seen by any candidate.

The material overleaf is provided for use in an emergency only (eg the recording or equipment proving faulty) or where permission has been given in advance by SQA for the material to be read to candidates with additional support needs. The material must be read exactly as printed.

Instructions to reader(s):

For each item, read the English **once**, then read the German **twice**, with an interval of 1 minute between the two readings. On completion of the second reading of Item Number One, pause for the length of time indicated in brackets after the item, to allow the candidates to write their answers.

Where special arrangements have been agreed in advance to allow the reading of the material, those sections marked **(f)** should be read by a female speaker and those marked **(m)** by a male; those sections marked **(t)** should be read by the teacher.

(t)   Item Number One

You listen to Sebastian talking on the radio about his school, which specialises in sport.

You now have one minute to study the questions for Item Number One.

(m) Seit drei Jahren gehe ich in eine Sportschule in meiner Heimatstadt. Ich habe mich für diese Schule beworben, weil ich mich sehr für Sport interessiere und später Sport studieren möchte.

Nach der schriftlichen Bewerbung hatte ich ein Vorstellungsgespräch, zu dem auch meine Eltern eingeladen wurden. Als ich meinen Platz bekam, war ich total glücklich.

Dennoch ist das Leben an einer Sportschule ziemlich anstrengend:

Mein Schultag beginnt sehr früh. Ich muss um sechs Uhr aufstehen, damit ich pünktlich um halb sieben in der Schwimmhalle bin. Jeden Morgen schwimme ich eine Stunde, bevor dann der Unterricht beginnt.

In der großen Pause laufen wir alle zwei Kilometer auf dem Sportplatz — auch wenn es regnet oder schneit. Und jeden Tag nach der Schule trainieren wir drei oder vier Stunden im Fitnessstudio und in der Sporthalle. Auch am Wochenende haben wir Training.

Trotzdem finde ich meine Schule super, weil die Lehrer sehr viel Zeit für die Schüler haben. Wenn wir Probleme haben, sind die Lehrer immer für uns da.

Obwohl wir dieselben Hauptfächer wie die Schüler in anderen Schulen haben, verbringen wir mehr Zeit mit Sport. Außerdem lernen wir sehr viel über gesunde Ernährung und wie man gesund kocht.

Am besten finde ich, dass jeden Monat bekannte Sportler in unsere Schule kommen und über ihre Erfahrungen sprechen. Sie bieten Trainingszeiten an, wo man nützliche Tipps bekommen und neue Techniken lernen kann.

Ich bin der Meinung, dass meine Schule ideal für mich ist, weil ich mein Talent entwickeln kann und die Möglichkeit habe, mich auf Sport zu spezialisieren.

(2 minutes)

(t) Item Number Two

Sebastian and his mother talk about school life at a boarding school.

You now have one minute to study the questions for Item Number Two.

(m) Sag mal, Mutti, du bist doch in Deutschland in eine Internatsschule gegangen. Warum?

(f) Meine Eltern — deine Großeltern — haben in verschiedenen Ländern der Welt gearbeitet. Sie waren zum Beispiel in Australien, Mexiko und Frankreich. Aber ich bin in Deutschland geblieben, weil ich ein deutsches Abitur haben wollte.

(m) Und wie hat dir das Leben in der Internatsschule gefallen?

(f) Zuerst war das gar nicht so einfach für mich. Natürlich habe ich meine Eltern vermisst. Aber dann habe ich meine Klassenkameraden besser kennen gelernt und viele neue Freunde gefunden. Meine Schule wurde schnell mein Zuhause, in dem ich mich sehr wohl gefühlt habe.

(m) Wie oft hast du deine Eltern gesehen?

(f) Naja, ich habe meine Eltern immer in den Schulferien gesehen — also viermal im Jahr. Ich bin dann zu ihnen ins Ausland gefahren. Außerdem habe ich sie auch getroffen, wenn sie in Deutschland waren. Das war immer schön.

(m) Und wie war der Schulalltag in deiner Schule?

(f) Normalerweise hatten wir acht Stunden pro Tag, denn der Schultag war länger als in den anderen Schulen. Außerdem hatten wir jeden Samstag Unterricht, weil wir längere Ferien hatten. Und natürlich gab es sehr viele Klubs und Vereine nach der Schule, damit wir keine Langeweile bekamen.

(m) Was war dein Lieblingsfach in der Schule?

(f) Ich muss sagen, dass ich schon immer sehr viel Spaß an Mathematik hatte, weil es ein logisches Fach ist. Musik oder Kunst waren nicht mein Fall. Da habe ich immer schlechte Noten bekommen.

(m) Und welche Sprachen musstest du in der Schule lernen?

(f) Ich habe Englisch und Französisch gelernt. Englisch hat mir aber besser gefallen, weil es jedes Jahr einen Schüleraustausch mit unserer Partnerschule in Aberdeen gab. Und deshalb bin ich in der zehnten Klasse für zwei Wochen nach Schottland gefahren — das hat richtig Spaß gemacht.

(m) Denkst du, dass Internatsschulen bessere Schulen sind?

(f) Hmmm, das würde ich nicht sagen. Internatsschulen sind sehr oft Schulen für Kinder, deren Eltern im Ausland arbeiten. Aber der Schulabschluss ist der gleiche — ob Internatsschule oder nicht. Und lernen muss man in jeder Schule, wenn man gute Noten und einen guten Abschluss haben will.

(m) Stimmt. Und deshalb mache ich jetzt lieber meine Hausaufgaben.

(f) Das ist eine gute Idee, Sebastian.

(t) End of recording.

[END OF TRANSCRIPT]

Page three

[BLANK PAGE]

DO NOT WRITE ON THIS PAGE

HIGHER

Answers

HIGHER GERMAN 2016

Reading

Question		Expected Answer(s)	Max mark
1		• It is the key to success. • They learn faster <u>and</u> better. *(Any 1 from 2)*	1
2		• Primary pupils are (fairly/quite) motivated. • (The same) secondary pupils are demotivated/lack motivation. • Secondary pupils don't apply themselves/make an effort (in class/lessons). *(Any 2 from 3)*	2
3		• To structure the syllabus/curriculum/teaching plan/learning plan/course/lesson<u>s</u>/tasks/work. • So that/to help/to encourage/to ensure pupils (make) progress/advance. • To motivate pupils. *(Any 2 from 3)*	2
4	a	She started truanting/skipping school/skiving (at age 14).	1
	b	• She had to swot/study/learn/cram (too many) facts. • The syllabus/curriculum/teaching plan/learning plan/course was/lesson<u>s</u> were <u>hardly ever</u> interesting.	2
5	a	• (Almost 40% of) children want <u>more</u> project work. • (1 in 5) wants it to be relevant/connected to daily life.	2
	b	An exciting story/exciting stories.	1
6		• They are fascinated by the digital world/have a fascination of the digital world. • They get to work with pictures/photos/videos/visuals <u>and</u> sound. • They can determine the level/standard for themselves. *(Any 2 from 3)*	2
7		• He would like to see more individual targets/aims/goals for pupils. • Lessons/teaching classes should be <u>more</u> flexible. • Pupils should (be able to) bring/contribute their own ideas and interests. *(Any 2 from 3)*	2

Question		Expected Answer(s)	Max mark
8	a	• Teachers don't have <u>enough</u> time <u>to plan</u> (lessons precisely). • They have <u>lots of/many other</u>/different things to organise. *(Any 1 from 2)*	1
	b	• <u>Not all</u> schools are equipped with modern technology/smart boards. *(Any 1 from 2)*	1
9		• Teenagers are <u>more</u> interested in life outside of school/their own lives./They have more interesting things in their lives outside of school. • Personal interest<u>s</u> (of pupils). • Motivation (of pupils). • Willingness/readiness to learn (of pupils). *(Any 1 from 4)*	1
10		<u>Outline of possible answers:</u> • Teachers are responsible for planning and structuring lessons appropriately/ensuring flexibility/personalisation. • Pupils have a responsibility to ensure that their outside interests do not affect their learning. • Schools are responsible for providing adequate modern resources/technology. • Lessons should be enjoyable/fun/interesting. <u>**Additional Guidance**</u> Markers must apply the following guidance in addition to the suggested Marking Instruction for this question:	2

Marks	Commentary
2	The candidate provides a clear answer, with justification that shows an accurate reading of the text. The answer clearly relates to the advice given in these Marking Instructions.
1	The candidate provides an answer which may contain some degree of misreading, but which offers evidence of some justification.
0	The candidate's answer simply provides information to be found in the text by simply re-stating answers to previous questions.

Question			Expected Answer(s)	Max mark
11			**Translation**	10
			„Spaß ist das Wichtigste im Klassenzimmer," meint Martina.	
			"Fun is the most important thing in the classroom," says Martina. *(2 marks)*	
			Die Schüler verlieren das Interesse,	
			The pupils lose interest, *(2 marks)*	
			wenn die Lernmethoden nicht abwechslungsreich sind.	
			if the learning methods are not varied. *(2 marks)*	
			Lehrer sollten den Unterricht vorsichtig planen,	
			Teachers should plan lessons carefully, *(2 marks)*	
			damit die Schüler am Ende ein Gefühl von Erfolg haben."	
			so that the pupils have a feeling of success at the end." *(2 marks)*	

Directed Writing

Candidates will write a piece of extended writing in German addressing a scenario that has four related bullet points. Candidates must address each bullet point. The first bullet point contains two pieces of information to be addressed. The remaining three bullet points contain one piece of information each. There is a choice of two scenarios and learners must choose one of these.

Mark	Content	Accuracy	Language resource: variety, range, structures
10	• The content is comprehensive • All bullet points are addressed fully and some candidates may also provide additional relevant information	• The language is accurate in all four bullets. However, where the candidate attempts to go beyond the range of the task, a slightly higher number of inaccuracies need not detract from the overall very good impression • A comprehensive range of verbs is used accurately and tenses are consistent and accurate • There is evidence of confident handling of all aspects of grammar and accurate spelling, although the language may contain a number of minor errors, or even one serious error • Where the candidate attempts to go beyond the range of the task, a slightly higher number of inaccuracies need not detract from the overall very good impression	• The language used is detailed and complex • There is good use of adjectives, adverbs, prepositional phrases and, where appropriate, word order • A comprehensive range of verbs/verb forms, tenses and constructions is used • Some modal verbs and infinitives may be used • The candidate is comfortable with the first person of the verb and generally uses a different verb in each sentence • Sentences are mainly complex and accurate • The language flows well

Mark	Content	Accuracy	Language resource: variety, range, structures
8	• The content is clear • All bullet points are addressed clearly. The response to one bullet point may be thin, although other bullet points are dealt with in some detail	• The language is mostly accurate. Where the candidate attempts to use detailed and complex language, this may be less successful, although basic structures are used accurately • A range of verbs is used accurately and tenses are generally consistent and accurate • There may be a few errors in spelling, adjective endings and, where relevant, case endings. Use of accents is less secure, where relevant	• The language used is detailed and complex • In one bullet point the language may be more basic than might otherwise be expected at this level • The candidate uses a range of verbs/verb forms and other constructions • There may be less variety in the verbs used • The candidate is comfortable with the first person of the verb and generally uses a different verb in each sentence • Sentences are generally complex and mainly accurate • Overall the writing will be very competent, essentially correct, but may be pedestrian
6	• The content is adequate and may be similar to that of an 8 • Bullet points may be addressed adequately, however **one** of the bullet points may not be addressed	• The language may be mostly accurate in two or three bullet points. However, in the remaining one or two, control of the language structure may deteriorate significantly • The verbs are generally correct, but basic • Tenses may be inconsistent, with present tenses being used at times instead of past tenses • There may be errors in spelling, adjective endings and some prepositions may be inaccurate or omitted. There are quite a few errors in other parts of speech — personal pronouns, gender of nouns, adjective endings, cases (where relevant), singular/plural confusion — and in the use of accents (where relevant) • Overall, there is more correct than incorrect and there is the impression that the candidate can handle tenses	• There are some examples of detailed and complex language • The language is perhaps repetitive and uses a limited range of verbs and fixed phrases not appropriate to this level • The candidate relies on a limited range of vocabulary and structures • There is minimal use of adjectives, probably mainly after "is" • The candidate has a limited knowledge of plurals • A limited range of verbs is used to address some of the bullet points • The candidate copes with the past tense of some verbs • When using the perfect tense, the past participle is incorrect or the auxiliary verb is omitted on occasion • Sentences are mainly single clause and may be brief
4	• The content may be limited and the Directed Writing may be presented as a single paragraph • Bullet points may be addressed in a limited way • **Two** of the bullet points are not be addressed	• The language is mainly inaccurate and after the first bullet the control of the language structure may deteriorate significantly. • A limited range of verbs is used • Ability to form tenses is inconsistent • In the use of the perfect tense the auxiliary verb is omitted on a number of occasions • There may be confusion between the singular and plural form of verbs • There are errors in many other parts of speech — gender of nouns, cases, singular/plural confusion — and in spelling and, where appropriate, word order • Several errors are serious, perhaps showing mother tongue interference	• There is limited use of detailed and complex language • The language is repetitive, with undue reliance on fixed phrases and a limited range of common basic verbs such as to be, to have, to play, to watch • The candidate mainly copes only with simple language • The verbs "was" and "went" may also be used correctly • Sentences are basic and there may be one sentence that is not intelligible to a sympathetic native speaker • An English word may appear in the writing or a word may be omitted • There may be an example of serious dictionary misuse

Mark	Content	Accuracy	Language resource: variety, range, structures
2	• The content may be basic or similar to that of a 4 or even a 6 • Bullet points are addressed with difficulty	• The language is inaccurate in all four bullets and there is little control of language structure • Many of the verbs are incorrect or even omitted. There is little evidence of tense control • There are many errors in other parts of speech — personal pronouns, gender of nouns, cases, singular/plural confusion, prepositions, for instance	• There is little use, if any, of detailed and complex language • Verbs used more than once may be written differently on each occasion • The candidate displays almost no knowledge of the past tense of verbs • The candidate cannot cope with more than one or two basic verbs • Sentences are very short and some sentences may not be understood by a sympathetic native speaker
0	• The content is very basic • The candidate is unable to address the bullet points Or • **Three or more** of the bullet points are not be addressed	• The language is seriously inaccurate in all four bullets and there is almost no control of language structure • Most errors are serious • Virtually nothing is correct • Very little is intelligible to a sympathetic native speaker	• There is no evidence of detailed and complex language • The candidate may only cope with the verbs to have and to be • There may be several examples of mother tongue interference. • English words are used • Very few words are written correctly in the modern language • There may be several examples of serious dictionary misuse

Section 1 — Listening

Item 1

Question		Expected Answer(s)	Max mark
1	a	• 17% of Germans live in a city (at the moment). • In 2030 19% of Germans will live in big cities. • In the next year_s/years_ to come, 12 million Germans will move (from the countryside) into towns. *(Any 1 from 3)*	1
	b	• <u>Better</u> work/job opportunities. • Career prospects/career chances. • Spare time is <u>more</u> interesting/There is more to do in your spare time/There are <u>more</u> interesting things to do in your spare time/Cities/The city are/is <u>better</u> for spending spare time. • There are cinema_s/restaurant_s/clubs/discos/sports club_s. *(3 for 1 point)* *(Any 2 from 4)*	2
	c	• Housing/houses/flats <u>and</u> houses/accommodation/property are/is expensive. • <u>Too many</u> cars (hinder the traffic) (in the city centre). • There are <u>not enough</u> kindergartens/nurseries/there are <u>too many</u> children for nurseries. • There are (often) <u>more than</u> 30 pupils in one class at school. *(Any 2 from 4)*	2

Question			Expected Answer(s)	Max mark
1	d	i	• There is a government programme in place. • (Germany spends) 10 million euros <u>per year</u> (on rural areas/the land). *(Any 1 from 2)*	1
		ii	• Improve quality of life. • (Not just) help for farmers/farming industry. • <u>More</u> (public) transport. • <u>More</u> supermarkets. • Faster/better internet (connection). *(Any 1 from 5)*	1
	e		Rural areas require significant development.	1

Item 2

Question		Expected Answer(s)	Max mark
2	a	• A big house <u>with a garden</u>. • Vanessa has a room of her own/does not have to share with her sister. • The family/They can have a dog (now). *(Any 1 from 3)*	1
	b	• She <u>loves</u> the city/cities/Berlin. • It is (much) <u>too</u> quiet for her (in the country). • It smells like cow/cow shed/cow dung./She cannot open her window <u>because of the smell</u>. *(Any 2 from 3)*	2

Question			Expected Answer(s)	Max mark

2	c		• Her mother finds life in Berlin/in a city strenuous/exhausting/tiring.
			• (Her mother has) problems with the number of cars/too many cars (in the city).
			  ◦ (Her mother has) has problems with the number of people/too many people (in the city).
			  ◦ (Mother) finds the city (quite) loud.
			  ◦ (Mother) finds the city dirty/polluted.
			(Any 2 details for 1 mark, 4 details for 2 marks)
			• Her father comes from a village.
			• Her father prefers to live in the country (to the town/city).
			(Any 2 from 4)
				2

	d	i	• Life in the country is ideal for her (job). • She has more/more than enough/plenty of/enough work in the countryside. • She is looking forward to working/can work with/there are horses, cows, sheep, pigs *(at least two animals for 1 point)*/big animals. • She rarely worked with big animals/these animals in Berlin. *(Any 2 from 4)*	2
		ii	• He works from home./He has an office in the basement/cellar. • He can concentrate better (because it is quiet).	2

Question		Expected Answer(s)	Max mark
2	e	• Berlin is (only) 10 kilometres away. • She did not have to change schools. • She goes to school/grammar school by bus./She gets the bus from school. • She visits her best friend at the weekend(s)./She is allowed to/can stay with her best friend over-night at weekend(s)./She can spend the weekend(s) with her best friend. • Her parents trust her. *(Any 2 from 5)*	2
	f	• Vanessa has (already) applied to (all four) Berlin universities/universities of Berlin/university in Berlin.	1

Section 2 — Writing

Candidates will write 120—150 words in a piece of extended writing in German addressing a stimulus of three questions in German.

Mark	Content	Accuracy	Language resource: variety, range, structures
10	• The content is comprehensive • The topic is addressed fully, in a balanced way • Some candidates may also provide additional information • Overall this comes over as a competent, well thought-out response to the task which reads naturally	• The language is accurate throughout. However where the candidate attempts to go beyond the range of the task, a slightly higher number of inaccuracies need not detract from the overall very good impression • A comprehensive range of verbs is used accurately and tenses are consistent and accurate • There is evidence of confident handling of all aspects of grammar and spelling accurately, although the language may contain a number of minor errors, or even one serious major error	• The language used is detailed and complex • There is good use of adjectives, adverbs, prepositional phrases and, where appropriate, word order • A comprehensive range of verbs/verb forms, tenses and constructions is used • Some modal verbs and infinitives may be used • The candidate is comfortable with the first person of the verb and generally uses a different verb in each sentence • The candidate uses co-ordinating conjunctions and subordinate clauses throughout the writing • Sentences are mainly complex and accurate • The language flows well

Mark	Content	Accuracy	Language resource: variety, range, structures
8	• The content is clear • The topic is addressed clearly	• The language is mostly accurate. However, where the candidate attempts to use detailed and complex language, this may be less successful, although basic structures are used accurately • A range of verbs is used accurately and tenses are generally consistent and accurate • There may be a few errors in spelling, adjective endings and, where relevant, case endings. Use of accents is less secure • Verbs and other parts of speech are used accurately but simply	• The language used is detailed and complex • The candidate uses a range of verbs/verb forms and other constructions • There may be less variety in the verbs used • The candidate is comfortable with the first person of the verb and generally uses a different verb in each sentence • Most of the more complex sentences use co-ordinating conjunctions, and there may also be examples of subordinating conjunctions where appropriate • Sentences are generally complex and mainly accurate • At times the language may be more basic than might otherwise be expected at this level • There may be an example of minor misuse of dictionary • Overall the writing will be very competent, essentially correct, but may be pedestrian
6	• The content is adequate and may be similar to that of an 8 or a 10 • The topic is addressed adequately	• The language may be mostly accurate. However, in places, control of the language structure may deteriorate significantly • The verbs are generally correct, but basic. Tenses may be inconsistent, with present tenses being used at times instead of past tenses • There may be errors in spelling, e.g. reversal of vowel combinations adjective endings and some prepositions may be inaccurate or omitted, e.g. I went the town. There are quite a few errors in other parts of speech — personal pronouns, gender of nouns, adjective endings, cases, singular/plural confusion — and in the use of accents • Overall, there is more correct than incorrect and there is the impression that the candidate can handle tenses	• There are some examples of detailed and complex language • The language is perhaps repetitive and uses a limited range of verbs and fixed phrases not appropriate to this level • The candidate relies on a limited range of vocabulary and structures • There is minimal use of adjectives, probably mainly after "is" • The candidate has a limited knowledge of plurals • The candidate copes with the present tense of most verbs • Where the candidate attempts constructions with modal verbs, these are not always successful • Sentences are mainly single clause and may be brief • There may be some dictionary misuse

Mark	Content	Accuracy	Language resource: variety, range, structures
4	• The content may be limited and may be presented as a single paragraph • The topic is addressed in a limited way	• The language used to address the more predictable aspects of the task may be accurate. However, major errors occur when the candidate attempts to address a less predictable aspect • A limited range of verbs is used • Ability to form tenses is inconsistent • In the use of the perfect tense the auxiliary verb is omitted on a number of occasions • There may be confusion between the singular and plural form of verbs • There are errors in many other parts of speech — gender of nouns, cases, singular/plural confusion — and in spelling and, where appropriate, word order • Several errors are serious, perhaps showing mother tongue interference • Overall there is more incorrect than correct	• There is limited use of detailed and complex language and the language is mainly simple and predictable • The language is repetitive, with undue reliance on fixed phrases and a limited range of common basic verbs such as to be, to have, to play, to watch • There is inconsistency in the use of various expressions, especially verbs • Sentences are basic and there may be one sentence that is not intelligible to a sympathetic native speaker • An English word may appear in the writing or a word may be omitted • There may be an example of serious dictionary misuse
2	• The content may be basic or similar to that of a 4 or even a 6 • The topic is thinly addressed	• The language is almost completely inaccurate throughout the writing and there is little control of language structure • Many of the verbs are incorrect or even omitted. There is little evidence of tense control • There are many errors in other parts of speech — personal pronouns, gender of nouns, cases, singular/plural confusion • Prepositions are not used correctly	• There is little use, if any, of detailed and complex language • The candidate has a very limited vocabulary • Verbs used more than once may be written differently on each occasion • The candidate cannot cope with more than one or two basic verbs • Sentences are very short and some sentences may not be understood by a sympathetic native speaker • Several English or "made-up" words may appear in the writing • There are examples of serious dictionary misuse
0	• The content is very basic • The candidate is unable to address the topic	• The language is seriously inaccurate throughout the writing and there is almost no control of language structure • (Virtually) nothing is correct • Most of the errors are serious • Very little is intelligible to a sympathetic native speaker	• There is no evidence of detailed and complex language • The candidate copes only with "have" and "am" • There may be several examples of mother tongue interference • Very few words are written correctly in the modern language • English words are used • There may be several examples of serious dictionary misuse

HIGHER GERMAN 2017

Reading

Question			Expected Answer(s)	Max mark
1			• <u>Every year</u> about 1·7 million kids/ young people go on holiday without their parents. • The market for youth trips/ travelling (at home and abroad) is <u>constantly</u> expanding. (Synonyms for constantly accepted) • The market for youth trips/ travelling (at home and abroad) has doubled <u>in the last five years</u>. *(Any 2 from 3)*	2
2			• Parents want/wish to have a quiet and relaxing holiday but/whereas/ while children want to have fun/ experience something exciting. (comparison is necessary in order to achieve the mark) • Parents are enthusiastic about a museum visit/can visit a museum <u>or</u> do a sightseeing tour (in a European metropolitan city) <u>but</u> children/young people find this boring. (comparison is necessary in order to achieve the mark) • On a family holiday it is often difficult to meet all expectations/ to be fair to everyone's expectations.	3
3			• They should find a travel agent/ agency (or any other acceptable phrase e.g. travel organiser) that specialises in youth trips/youth travelling. • They should ask themselves if their child is mature enough/ready to travel <u>on their own/in a group.</u> • They should consider that there are different types of holidays/which holiday is the right one (for the child). • Discuss with child if a skiing holiday in France/a language holiday in England/a holiday camp on the Baltic is the right holiday for them. **2 places required, including type of holiday and country for 1 mark.** *(Any 3 from 4)*	3
4	a		• She must find out what parents <u>and</u> children expect (from the trip). • She must find out how much money parents can/want to spend (on the trip). *(Any 1 from 2)*	1
	b		• The (possible) fears/worries/ concerns that <u>parents</u> have. • (Since birth) their child has always been close to them and then suddenly their son/daughter wants to go on holiday with a youth group. *(Any 1 from 2)*	1
5			• (It's not just about) individual holidays, where everyone can pursue their own interests/you can do the things that interest you. • Children and young people learn to live <u>and</u> cooperate in a group. • They are together with their peers. • They have the chance to develop themselves (freely)/to find new <u>friends</u>/to experience great things. *(Any 3 from 4)*	3
6	a		• He learned/experienced things which he cannot learn/experience in his <u>daily life/in Berlin</u>. • Watch the sunrise (in the mornings) at the sea/sleep on the beach/ sit around the campfire in the evenings/with other young people. **2 examples required for 1 mark.** • He met <u>many</u> new <u>people</u>. • (Next year) he wants to travel <u>abroad</u>/go on an adventure holiday <u>to Norway</u> (with a youth group). *(Any 3 from 4)*	3
	b		• (In the first few days) his mother <u>constantly</u> phoned him. • His mother texted him <u>at least</u> ten times. • He missed his family <u>a little</u>. *(Any 2 from 3)*	2
7			<u>Outline of possible answers:</u> • Yes: personal development, opportunities to socialise, becoming young adults. • No: not for everyone, depends on the level of maturity, homesickness. • Yes, but there could be some issues with homesickness and the type of holiday. <u>Additional Guidance:</u> A mark of 2, 1 or 0 will be awarded for this question. Markers should follow this advice:	2

Question			Expected Answer(s)		Max mark
			Marks	**Commentary**	
			2	The candidate provides a clear answer, with justification that shows an accurate reading of the text. The answer clearly relates to the advice given in the "Expected answer(s)" column.	
			1	The candidate provides an answer that may contain some degree of misreading, but that offers evidence of some justification.	
			0	The candidate's answer provides information to be found in the text by simply re-stating answers to previous questions.	
8			Translation		10
			Zu Hause in vertrauter Umgebung		
			At home/In the house in familiar surroundings/a familiar environment		
			(2 marks)		
			In familiar surrounds trusted/trustworthy/trusting a surrounding		
			(1 mark)		
			Close surroundings		
			(0 marks)		
			treffen die Eltern oft Entscheidungen für ihre Kinder.		
			(the) parents often make decisions for their children.		
			(2 marks)		
			Adults/Decide for/The decision		
			(1 mark)		
			Meet decisions		
			Their child		
			(0 marks)		
			Wenn Kinder ohne ihre Eltern in ein Feriencamp fahren,		
			If/when children go/travel to/on (a) holiday camp without their parents,		
			(2 marks)		
			Omission of ihre		
			(1 mark)		
			A child		
			<u>Are</u> on/at a holiday camp		
			(0 marks)		
			müssen sie selbst Verantwortung tragen.		
			they must/have to take/bear responsibility (for) themselves.		
			(2 marks)		

Question			Expected Answer(s)	Max mark
			Omission of selbst	
			Take self-responsibility	
			<u>Be</u> responsible/<u>have</u> responsibility for themselves bear their own responsibility	
			(1 mark)	
			Responsibilities	
			Carry/wear	
			(0 marks)	
			In vielen Fällen macht diese Erfahrung Jugendliche stärker und selbstbewusster.	
			In many/a lot of cases, this experience makes young people stronger and more confident/self-assured.	
			(2 marks)	
			No comparative	
			Plural of noun + verb, <u>IF the rest of the sentence is correct.</u>	
			young person.	
			(1 mark)	
			In many ways	
			(0 marks)	

Directed Writing

Please refer back to pp. 92–94 for further advice on the General Marking Principles for Higher German Directed Writing.

Section 1 — Listening

Item 1

Question		Expected Answer(s)	Max mark
1	a	• (In 2030) 70% of people will be older than/over 30.	1
	b	• Fewer children are being born. • Families have (only) one or (maximum) two children. • A healthy lifestyle is (very) <u>important</u> (for many Germans). • <u>Modern</u> medicine/medication (helps to treat illnesses better). *(Any 3 from 4)*	3
	c i	• More flats/homes/housing <u>specially</u> <u>designed/adapted/suitable</u> (for older people) must be built.	1
	ii	• Germany will need more nurses <u>and</u> social workers. • Germany must look for staff abroad (if they cannot find staff in the country). *(Any 1 from 2)*	1
	d	• Ideal model for the job market (of the future). • <u>Europeans/People in Europe</u> have the right to live/work in any EU country. • Easier to solve (present and future) problems (together). *(Any 2 from 3)*	2

Item 2

Question			Expected Answer(s)	Max mark
2	a		• He has lived there for six months. • It is in the town/city centre. • It is <u>relatively/pretty/fairly</u> big/large. • It has a <u>wonderful</u> (or any synonym) garden. • The garden has benches **and** (many) trees. *(Any 2 from 5)*	2
	b		• There is a hobby room/common room/spare time/free time room. • (Where) they play cards/video games. • <u>Every week</u>, they <u>organise</u> a shopping day **or** Every week they go <u>together</u> to the supermarket/shopping (by bus). *(Any 2 from 3)*	2
	c		• Everything is voluntary/optional/nobody has to join in/nobody has to do something they don't want to do.	1
	d	i	• He can learn from his elderly/older neighbours/elders. • He can ask them if he has a problem ('them' must refer to the older neighbours). • Older people don't have to live on their own. • Younger neighbours are there for older neighbours. *(Any 2 from 4)*	2
		ii	• You should not be **too** loud/noisy. • When listening to music, put the headphones on/use the headphones. • Have (wild) parties at the disco **or** Don't have (wild) parties at home. *(Any 2 from 3)*	2
	e		• They take mail out of the letter box/collect his post. • They water the flowers/plants. • They feed his cat. *(Any 1 from 3)*	1
	f		• Robert wanted to live in/have his own flat/place/home <u>in the town centre/town/city centre/city</u>. • Robert does not like to be/live on his own **or** He is a sociable/social person.	2

Section 2 — Writing

Please see pp. 95—97 for the general marking principles for Higher German Writing.

Reading

Question			Expected Answer(s)	Max mark
1			• <u>More than half</u> of young Spaniards/young people (in Spain)/young Spanish people (between 15—24) have no job in their own country/Spain/there is no work for them in Spain	1
2	a		• (He is doing) an apprenticeship/(job) training <u>at a construction firm</u> • He <u>never</u> had a (permanent/firm) contract (in Spain) • He <u>was made/became</u> redundant/unemployed/lost job (in Spain) *(Any 2 from 3)* *Note: Answers from 2b are not accepted for 2a*	2
	b		• He is not homesick/no homesickness/<u>Only</u> misses his mother's cooking • He has better <u>job</u> opportunities/prospects/<u>professional</u> chances <u>in Germany</u> (at the moment) (singular accepted as appropriate) • He would <u>probably</u> be unemployed (again) in Spain • His family would have to support him financially *(Any 2 from 4)*	2
3	a		• Because there is a lack of <u>skilled</u> workers (in Germany)	1
	b		• They (normally) come with/have experience/are experienced • They speak <u>at least</u> two <u>other/foreign/modern</u> languages	2
4			• They work for the same company/firm • They did the same intensive <u>German</u> language course <u>in Spain</u> • They live in the same street (in Heidelberg)	3
5	a		• (One/She/you) cannot <u>live</u> off the salary/pay/money you get	1
	b		• She <u>misses</u> her/the (familiar) language • She <u>misses</u> the (Spanish) cuisine/food/cooking • She <u>misses</u> the (typical Spanish) festiva<u>ls</u>/celebration<u>s</u>/part<u>ies</u> with <u>friends and family</u> *(Any 2 from 3)*	2

n	Expected Answer(s)	Max mark
	• Many want to start/have/ establish their own family (in Spain) • Their/the boyfriend(s)/ girlfriend(s) does not <u>want</u> to come to Germany *(Any 1 from 2)*	1
7	• Support them to look for a <u>suitable</u> flat/apartment • A company car <u>after a 3 month probationary period</u> (which you can use for private purposes) • <u>Annual/yearly</u> pay rise (paid on time) • Finance/pay for the annual holiday to (visit family in) <u>Spain</u> *(Any 2 from 4)*	2
8	• (So far) the situation in Spain has not changed/improved/is not changing	1
9	**Positive:** • Gaps in workforce • Healthy job market/vacancies • Support for them eg language courses, integration support • Financial benefits/more money **Negative:** • Miss the culture • Don't want to start a family away from home • Language barrier • Brain drain in Spain/young people leaving their home country Or a balanced view **Additional Guidance:** A mark of 2, 1 or 0 will be awarded for this question. Markers should follow this advice: | Marks	Commentary
---	---
2	The candidate provides a clear answer, with justification that shows an accurate reading of the text. The answer clearly relates to the advice given in the 'Expected answer(s)' column.
1	The candidate provides an answer that may contain some degree of misreading, but that offers evidence of some justification.
0	The candidate's answer provides information to be found in the text by simply re-stating answers to previous questions.		2

Question	Expected Answer(s)	Max mark
10	**Translation** **„Am Anfang hatte ich große Schwierigkeiten mit der deutschen Sprache,** "At/In the beginning/At the start/ To begin/start with I had great difficulties with the German language, *(2 marks)* Big/huge Difficulty Omission of the *(1 mark)* My German speaking German *(0 marks)* **obwohl meine Kollegen sehr hilfsbereit und verständnisvoll waren.** although/even though my colleagues were very helpful and understanding. *(2 marks)* however ready to help omission of very *(1 mark)* colleague was *(0 marks)* **Viele Deutsche sprechen mit einem starken Akzent,** Many/Lots of/A lot of Germans/ German people speak with a strong/thick accent, *(2 marks)* Accents Omission of a *(1 mark)* Are speaking/spoke German speakers *(0 marks)* **der für mich schwierig zu verstehen war.** Which/that was difficult/hard for me to understand. *(2 marks)* Omission of for me For me that/this is hard to understand *(1 mark)* Complete omission of relative pronoun is difficult/made it difficult stand *(0 marks)*	10

Question			Expected Answer(s)	Max mark
			Außerdem musste ich die Grammatik gründlich studieren."	
			Moreover/furthermore/In addition/Additionally apart from that/besides I had to study the grammar thoroughly." *(2 marks)*	
			Also Omission of the *(1 mark)*	
			Omission of moreover Anyway Must/have to Learn *(0 marks)*	

Directed Writing

Please refer back to pp. 92–94 for further advice on the General Marking Principles for Higher German Directed Writing.

Section 1 — Listening

Item 1

Question		Expected Answer(s)	Max mark
1	a	• He had to do a (written) application • He had to do an interview	2
	b	• (school) day starts early/gets up at 6am • Be at the swimming pool at 6.30 • Swims (for an hour) <u>before</u> lessons begin/school/his day starts • Run <u>2km</u> at break/lunch break/lunch • <u>After school</u> they train for <u>3–4 hours</u> • Training at the weekend(s) *(Any 3 from 6)*	3
	c	• They have <u>lots of/a lot of</u> time for the pupils • The teachers are (always) <u>there if/when pupils have a problem</u> *(Any 1 from 2)*	1
	d	• They have the same core/main subjects • <u>Healthy</u> diet/nutrition/eating • How to cook <u>healthily</u> *(Any 1 from 3)*	2

Question		Expected Answer(s)	Max mark
	e	• (famous) sports people/athlete(s) come to the school to talk (about their experiences) **or** (famous) sports people/athlete(s) come to the school to offer training sessions **or** pupils can get <u>useful</u> tips/<u>new</u> techniques *NOTE: Answer must imply tips/ techniques come from the sports person.* • He can develop his talent • He has the opportunity/is able to specialise in sports *(Any 1 from 3)*	

Item 2

Question		Expected Answer(s)	Max mark
2	a	• Her parents/Sebastian's grandparents <u>worked</u> in different countries/all over the world/abroad **or** Her parents/ Sebastian's grandparents <u>worked</u> in Australia, Mexico and France (all 3 countries must be mentioned) • She <u>wanted</u> to get her (German) Abitur/a <u>German</u> (school) qualification	2
	b	• It wasn't easy <u>at first</u> • She missed her parents/family • She got to know her classmates/ made/met/found new friends • She felt at ease/happy there/ the school soon/quickly became her home *(Any 2 from 4)*	2
	c	• She saw them always in the holidays/every (school) holiday/ four times a year in the holidays *NOTE: "frequency of" + "holiday(s)" mentioned = 2 marks* *If only 1 element mentioned = 1 mark* • When the parents/they were in Germany	2

n	Expected Answer(s)	Max mark
	• 8 lessons/periods <u>per day</u> • School day was longer <u>than other schools</u> • Lessons/classes on Saturdays/a Saturday • Clubs <u>after school</u> *(Any 2 from 4)*	2
e	• She learnt/had to learn French <u>and</u> English • She <u>preferred</u> English/<u>liked</u> English better • She took part in/went on a school exchange (for two weeks/to Aberdeen/Scotland) **or** She went to Scotland/Aberdeen for two weeks with the school/on a school trip *NOTE: Answer must imply that it was Sebastian's mother who went on the trip/exchange* *(Any 2 from 3)*	2

Question		Expected Answer(s)	Max mark
f		• They are schools for children whose parents <u>work</u> abroad • The leaving exam/qualification at the end is the same • You have to learn/study/work in every/any school (to get good grades) *(Any 2 from 3)*	2

Section 2 — Writing

Please see pp. 95—97 for the general marking principles for **Higher German Writing**.

Acknowledgements

Permission has been sought from all relevant copyright holders and Hodder Gibson is grateful for the use of the following:

Text adapted from www.br-online.de/kinder/fragen-verstehen/klaro/lupe/2006/01374/ © Bayerischer Rundfunk (2018 Listening Transcript pages 2 & 3)